Life

Is

Spiritual

Daily Power Series

Michael Burns

Life Is Spiritual—Walking through 1 Corinthians
Daily Power Series
© 2024 by Michael Burns

ISBN: 978-1-958723-18-0. Printed in the United States.

Illumination Publishers cares deeply about the environment and uses recycled paper whenever possible.

All Scripture quotations, unless indicated, are taken from the Holy Bible, New International Version (NIV), copyright © 2011, 2015 by Biblica, Inc. Used by permission. All rights reserved.

Scriptures marked NASB are taken from the New American Standard Bible (NASB), copyright ©1960, 1971, 1977, 1995, and 2020 by The Lockman Foundation. All rights reserved.

Cover design and interior layout by Toney C. Mulhollan. Copyediting by Amy Morgan.

Theatron Press is an imprint of Illumination Publishers and titles may be purchased in bulk for classroom instruction, business, fundraising, or sales promotional use. For additional information please email paul.ipibooks@me.com.

About the author: Michael Burns (DMin Bethel University; MA Wesley Seminary, Indiana Wesleyan University) is the Congregational Teacher for the DFW Church in Dallas-Fort Worth, Texas. He is the cohost of the Eikon Podcast. His other books include *Crossing the Line: Culture, Race, and Kingdom; All Things to All People: The Power of Cultural Humility*; and *Escaping the Beast: Politics, Allegiance, and Kingdom.* He and his wife, MyCresha, have two adult children. All of Michael's books are available for purchase at www.ipibooks.com.

*Theatron Press is an imprint of
Illumination Publishers International*

*Since we live by the Spirit,
let us keep in
step with the Spirit.*

—the Apostle Paul[1]

1. Galatians 5:25

Contents

Contents

Introduction

Welcome to the interactive quiet time booklet that is designed to study and apply the letter of 1 Corinthians, *Life Is Spiritual.* This is a 40-day devotional book that walks through Paul's letter to the church in the city of Corinth. Each day follows a similar pattern of sections, which are explained below. We hope that this devotional series serves as an encouraging and helpful means of assistance to help you as the Holy Spirit guides you through our collective study of the book of 1 Corinthians.

Scripture and Day

Each day of this series is numbered separately and contains a specific passage of Scripture that you will be studying for that day. Passages are sequential and will cover every verse in the letter of 1 Corinthians. You will get the most from this series if you do not skip any days. If you miss a day for any reason, our suggestion is to simply cover that day in the devotional in your next quiet time and go from there, or you could cover two days in the devotional in your next quiet time. Following the series for forty straight days is the most effective option, however.

Quotation

Each day begins with a quotation from an early church leader that pertains directly to the passage being studied that day. Most of the quotations come from Christians writing in the second, third, and fourth centuries. These ancient writings are not authoritative as Scripture is, but they offer a wonderful insight into how our brothers and sisters of the past lived out the truth of the Scriptures in their own context. In that light, the quotes can be very helpful. Plus, it is encouraging and productive to hear the perspectives and voices of others rather than just being limited to our contemporary context.

Read

In the "Read" section you are asked to read the passage for that day aloud and then again slowly and silently to focus on the words you are reading. It is recommended that you consider reading in each manner more than once, but that is optional. If you do read either aloud or to yourself more than once, you may want to read in a different translation each time to give you a broader feel for the text.

Reflect – A Thought of Reflection

The "A Thought of Reflection" section is not an exhaustive commentary. This section is optional but encouraged. It is designed simply as a summary of some of the main points of the Scripture reading for that day as well as giving some historical and cultural background and context to aid in better understanding the passage. For greater depth, you may wish to consult a quality commentary in addition to this series.

Reflect – Preparation for Reflection

This section is also optional but encouraged. It guides the participant in probing a bit deeper in thought through questions in areas such as the meaning of the text, the motivations behind the text, or the motivations of the participant. These questions can be answered as part of the participant's thought process, or they can be written down.

Recite

For the "Recite" section, a small portion of the passage for that day was selected as the focus of a short period of meditation. You might think about the phrase and wrestle with its meanings and applications. You might think about it and listen for the Holy Spirit to guide you into a deeper understanding of how that phrase can interact with and transform your life. Or you may choose to audibly repeat the phrase over and over with an ear for the guidance and revelation of the Spirit. Make this section your own—find what works best for you, recognizing that it may be one technique, or it might work better to change it up a bit each day. You might also decide to select a different phrase on any given day and substitute it for the one suggested. This section is optional but encouraged.

Respond

Each day there are three short prayer prompts provided. This is designed to assist you in connecting that day's passage with your prayers. You may add the prompts to your prayer time. Or you may decide to craft your prayers based on the reading or not do so at all. This section is optional but encouraged.

The Remainder of the Week

The resources in this section are provided for those who will find them helpful or useful. Because this is a daily devotional series, participants may find it overwhelming to keep up with all elements of this section for the entire week. You may choose to utilize each section for a day or an entire week. The "Questions for Reflection" and "Application" sections are designed to aid you in putting these passages into action within the life of your church body and in your own life.

Each day contains an *academic article* or *video link*. These are completely optional and only encouraged for those who are stimulated by academic and deeper thought. Because most of the articles linked in this section are academic in nature, they can be a little more challenging to access. Some articles are direct links. A few require a sign-up process, library, or educational institution access, and one requires a small fee. Where the full and free article was available online directly, that link is provided. Some may require a bit of work on your part to access.

1 CORINTHIANS 1:1–17

If human wisdom is at war with the cross and fights against the gospel, it is not right to boast about it. Rather, we should recoil in shame.
                    —Chrysostom, 4th century AD

READ

—Read 1 Corinthians 1:1–17 out loud at least once.
—Read 1 Corinthians 1:1–17 at least once silently to yourself. Read it very slowly, allowing time for each word and phrase to resonate.

REFLECT

A Thought of Reflection

Much like a newly married person who can't stop mentioning their spouse, Paul cannot keep the name of "Christ" off his lips. For him, Christ is the embodiment and definition of everything to which they are called to be as a people. That means that they are not just to respond to the gospel message but to learn to inhabit it and become it. This will challenge every part of their life together and their lives as individuals. They are about to discover that there is nothing that lies separate from the way of the cross. Everything is spiritual.

Paul has something very specific in mind for confronting divisions. He doesn't refer to mere disagreements among them. Rather, he recognizes that their cultural instinct is to allow or create hierarchical levels based on social status. In short, they were allowing the cultural practices around them and the effects of those mindsets and practices to become normal in the life of the church. Roman culture was prone to develop identity, status, and worth based on which ideology, philosophy, or teacher one followed. They then split into factions, each group believing themselves to be superior in intellect and status to the others. In Christ, we are to be a new-creation people. We must understand that we are all created as image-bearers of God, with that as our sole identity. That means no division, no primary identities that separate us. All that matters is Christ.

To mimic the culture here was doubly dangerous. It allowed the divisions of society to work their way into the church. That was bad enough. But it also meant that the equality of image bearing in Christ was destroyed among them. They were no longer the new creation. Giving room for any ideology, philosophy, political belief, allegiance, or identity to define ourselves or others is to deform the community that is crafted by God to take the shape of the cross.

Preparation for Reflection

1. How many times does Paul refer to Christ in the first ten verses? In a letter that centers on divisions and challenges a church that has given room for cultural identities, status, and values to exist in the church, what is so important about Paul beginning this letter by bringing up Christ repeatedly?

2. Before we move on as Paul begins to lay out his reasons for why divisions and cultural hierarchies based on status are so contrary to the gospel, why do you think they are so destructive to a cross-shaped community?

3. Paul contends that he will not follow the cultural patterns of expounding his message through impressive rhetoric and gaining a large following but will instead "preach" the gospel by embodying the way of the cross. Given that, what do you think he meant by warning against the cross of Christ being emptied of its power?

RECITE

 Take 2–3 minutes to meditate on your own on the phrase, "that there be no divisions among you." Listen for the Spirit to reveal new insights of understanding and application of this phrase to your life.

RESPOND

As you move into a time of prayer, focus on the things you normally pray for but today take some time to pray:

- that God's people will examine the aspects of culture that deeply influence and draw us away from taking the shape of the cross of Christ as a community.

- that God will unite us and keep us from division.

- specifically for those who have allowed themselves to harbor other allegiances and identities. Pray that you will love them graciously and that they may be drawn to Christ alone.

THE REMAINDER OF THE WEEK

Questions for Reflection

- What are some of the cultural assumptions and structures that can work their way into the life of the church that I may have continued to accept without examination?

- Are there any ways that I have contributed to division in the body of Christ?

Application

- What is an application that you take away from this section for your faith community?

- What is the personal application that you take away from this section?

Further Study (Optional)

- Read the following article about social structure in ancient Corinth: (PDF) The Social Background of 1 Corinthians 1–4 (researchgate.net).

https://www.researchgate.net/publication/334591037_The_Social_Background_of_1_Corinthians_1-4

1 CORINTHIANS 1:18–31

The power and wisdom of God are not the divinity of Christ as such but the preaching of the cross.
— Theodore of Mopsuestia, 5th century AD

READ

—Read 1 Corinthians 1:18–31 out loud at least once.
—Read 1 Corinthians 1:18–31 at least once silently to yourself. Read it very slowly, allowing time for each word and phrase to resonate in your heart.

REFLECT

A Thought of Reflection

Genesis 1 tells us that God created all human beings to be his image-bearers, meaning that we were to equally reflect his will, character, and purposes into the world as his representatives. Genesis 3 recounts how the Serpent convinced humans that they were superior to that purpose and could be more than image-bearers. Sadly, while humanity was created to equally represent God and live in harmony, they seized upon the lie that they were superior, but there is always a cost to sin. Chasing this lie resulted in the superiority of some, but the subjugation and treatment of many others as inferior. This was the exact opposite of what communities of image-bearers were to be; and the vocation of image-bearing humans was lost. It was not until Jesus came that we again see a true image-bearer (Col. 1:15; 2 Corinthians 4:4). Part of the gospel's good news is that in Christ, humans are being restored to the role of image-bearers (2 Corinthians 3:18).

Since the Serpent's original law of superiority to the calling of image bearing, human cultures and societies have fallen prey to one version or another of that law and constructed systems and structures that treated some as superior and others as inferior. One of the most prevalent versions of that lie in the Roman Empire was that those with high social status were exceptional and deserved more rights, freedom, and privileges. They were the wise, the noble, the strong, and they boasted, or established their identity, as superior wherever they could. Their whole society was constructed around this lie of human identity and worth.

Contrasting that, the gospel did not appeal to or derive from this kind of human wisdom. It was a humble message crafted on the idea that the true King had suffered for the benefit of others and called them to live out this way of the cross. Rather than life being about exalting their status, it was about laying their lives down for others. A crucified king was a troubling idea for Jews waiting for a victorious Messiah but seemed utterly ridiculous to the Greek and Roman culture of power and superiority. Paul's primary point in this passage is not to simply criticize the world but to demonstrate the folly of those in Christ who had not carefully examined the full implications of being image-bearers in Christ and were now trying to smuggle into the life of the church the wisdom of human society and the injustice, inequity, and other effects of rejecting true image bearing. The only thing that establishes our identity, says Paul, is our status in Christ. That is the only foundation upon which we should rightly order our lives together as God's people. Yet he will go on to show them that they have been doing quite the opposite. This is a stern reminder for us because we are just as susceptible to our versions of the lie of superiority as the Corinthians were to theirs.

Preparation for Reflection

1. Why do you think Paul intentionally points out that God often uses those of low status and identity rather than the elites and impressive people?

2. Given that Paul is about to challenge the church for allowing the lie of superiority and the effects of social status and hierarchy into the church, why does he remind them that most of them were not of elite status according to the wisdom of their culture?

3. Remembering that boasting was specifically the concept of establishing one's identity and social worth, what are the implications of Paul telling believers that they have no boast except for being in Christ? What impact would that have on the way they interact with one another?

RECITE

Take 2–3 minutes to meditate on your own on the phrase, "Let the one who boasts boast in the Lord." Listen to the Spirit to reveal new insights of understanding and application of this phrase in your life.

RESPOND

As you move into a time of prayer, focus on the things you normally pray for but today take some time to pray:

- that God's people will wrestle with the countercultural ideas of living out the way of the cross and being his true image-bearers.
- that he will help us be a church that truly takes the shape of the cross in our individual and collective lives.
- specifically for those impacted by the lies, injustice, and inequities of the world to see their true identity in Christ and experience the reality of that in the life of the church.

THE REMAINDER OF THE WEEK

Questions for Reflection

- Are there ways that we establish our identity and worth other than the equalizing ground at the foot of the cross and being in Christ?

Application

- What is an application that you take away from this section for your faith community?
- What is the personal application that you take away from this section?

Further Study (Optional)

- Read the following article about image bearing: Our Collective Image-Bearing Mission: Do You Accept? | *Artios Magazine.*

https://baonline.org/image-bearing-mission/#:~:text=The%20vocation...%20 is%20that%20of%20being%20a%20genuine,praises%20of%20all%20 creation%20back%20to%20its%20maker.

1 CORINTHIANS 2:1–5

If our Scriptures had persuaded people to believe be-cause they had been written with rhetorical art or phil-osophical skill, there is no doubt that our faith would be said to depend on the art of words and human wisdom rather than on the power of God.

—Origen, 3rd century AD

READ

—Read 1 Corinthians 2:1–5 out loud at least once.

—Read 1 Corinthians 2:1–5 at least once silently to your-self. Read it very slowly, allowing time for each word and phrase to resonate in your heart.

REFLECT

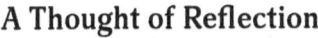

A Thought of Reflection

When Daniel and the other exiles first arrived in Baby-lon, they suddenly found themselves surrounded by the wisdom, power, impressiveness, and might of the most successful empire in the world at the time. The pressure to be in-fluenced and transformed by its wisdom was enormous. Babylon had just decimated Israel and was the most powerful force in the Ancient Near East, so what they were doing worked. But Daniel and his friends needed to remind themselves that the world's wisdom, success, and provision are not all they are cracked up to be. So, for a temporary period at the beginning of their exile, they abstained from the impressive menu of the king's table and put themselves in the hands of God alone. This wasn't about a better diet; it was to remind them of the source of true wisdom.

The Corinthians faced a similar problem. They had not been dragged into exile in a foreign land, but as people of the new creation who were living in the present age, they were to become the embodiment of the gospel, living with Jesus as King according to God's wisdom. One aspect of this reality was to be an image-bearing community with no status or hierarchies of superiority such as free over slave, Gentile over Jew (or vice versa), male over female, and so on. This meant examining carefully and rejecting the systems of the culture around them and righting many of the sinful wrongs and inequities created by those systems. To do this, they must resist the wisdom of the world and see its flaws.

The humble way of the cross is counter to the world's wisdom. It is not just the good news of forgiveness and reconciliation made available to all humans because of Jesus' sacrifice on the cross. It is the call to embody the cross and, as a community, take up its shape in the way we live. This was not a popular message in Paul's day, just as it is not in ours. The problem is that, while we might celebrate Jesus' work on the cross, when it comes to embodying the way of the cross in our own lives, it looks powerless, ineffective, dangerous, and just plain stupid. We can very subtly become formed by the wisdom of this age to believe that although as Christians, we know what justice truly is, we must have power and influence to enact that just and righteous life. But God's power is nothing more and nothing less than the way of the cross. And that can be a hard pill to swallow in the reality of daily life surrounded by a world that views it as nonsense.

Preparation for Reflection

1. What is the importance of the cross in your life?

2. What does it mean for a church community to become cross shaped?

3. What are some of the powerful forces in our culture and society other than the cross that can have a transformational effect on our beliefs, ideologies, presumptions, and actions?

RECITE

Take 2–3 minutes to meditate on the phrase, "I resolved to know nothing...except Jesus Christ and him crucified." Listen for the Spirit to reveal new understanding and application of this phrase in your life.

RESPOND

As you move into a time of prayer, focus on the things you normally pray for but today take some time to pray:

- that your church will grow ever more discerning when it comes to being aware of the influences of worldly wisdom and cultural discipling.

- that God will help us to be resolved to know nothing but Jesus Christ and the way of the cross.

- for those who don't know the cross and are still enslaved to the wisdom of the world. But make sure as you pray for them that no judgment or condescension sneaks into your heart.

THE REMAINDER OF THE WEEK

Questions for Reflection

- What are some sources of worldly wisdom that you take in that might merit further examination and discernment?

- What does it mean for your life to be cross shaped?

Application

- What is an application that you take away from this section for your faith community?

- What is the personal application that you take away from this section?

Further Study (Optional)

- Read the following article about what it means to say that the Bible and its wisdom are authoritative: How Can the Bible Be Authoritative? –NTWrightPage.

https://ntwrightpage.com/2016/07/12/how-can-the-bible-be-authoritative/

1 CORINTHIANS 2:6-13

DAY 4

The mature are those who preach the cross as wisdom because of the witness of Christ's power at work. They know that actions speak louder than words. Their wisdom is not of this age but of the age to come.

—Ambrosiaster, 4th century AD

READ

—Read 1 Corinthians 2:6–13 out loud at least once.

—Read 1 Corinthians 2:6–13 at least once silently to yourself. Read it very slowly, allowing time for each word and phrase to resonate.

REFLECT
A Thought of Reflection

For Paul, the "rulers of this age," is a reference to what he elsewhere calls the rulers and authorities (Ephesians 6:12), the powers of this dark world (Eph. 6:12), the spiritual forces of evil in the heavenly realms (Eph. 6:12), the elemental spiritual forces of the world (Gal. 4:3; Col. 2:8), etc. They were part of the divine realm that had been created by God to shepherd the nations toward him in unified image bearing but had instead rebelled against God and now work to sow division and conflict at the level of societies, nations, cultures, systems, structures, ideologies, philosophies, and so on. Wherever Paul is addressing unity or division among the believers, a mention of the powers and authorities is not far behind. They cannot be allowed to operate in the church the way they do in the rest of the world.

So, when Paul breaks into his discussion here concerning spiritual wisdom and worldly wisdom, we must avoid the temptation to interpret that in an overly religious and abstract manner. The deep practicality with which Paul addresses the Corinthians is simple: When they allow the divisions and inequities of the world to operate in the church, they are exalting human wisdom. Spiritually mature wisdom goes no further than the way of the cross. This wisdom doesn't mean they blindly or naively believe that they are all now equal simply because they believe in Christ. Rather, it is the understanding that all image-bearers are equal, but they have been trained and sorted by a system of superiority and inferiority their whole lives and must now actively and intentionally live in a very different way. This is the way of the new creation.

When the powers and authorities worked through and with their human counterparts to crucify Jesus, they thought they had won, but they did not understand the power of the cross. What seems like foolishness and defeat is the wisdom of God to bring about true victory and real change. This is not just a religious theory for Paul. The cross is a tangible life that must be chosen, implemented, and lived out consistently if God's people are to escape the enslavement of the powers of this age.

Preparation for Reflection

1. What was going on in the Corinthian church that led Paul to the conclusion that they were operating under the influence of the powers and authorities?

2. What does Paul say is the only means through which they will be able to access the mind and wisdom of God as a people?

3. Paul's point is not that they need to engage in some showy exorcisms or spiritual warfare to defeat the work of the powers among them. Rather, they need to simply focus on living by the wisdom of God. Why do you think Paul directs them to live differently rather than solely praying for delivery?

RECITE

Take 2–3 minutes to meditate on your own on the phrase, "None of the rulers of this age understood [God's wisdom]." Listen for the Spirit to reveal new insights of understanding and application of this phrase in your life.

RESPOND

As you move into a time of prayer, focus on the things you normally pray for but today take some time to pray:

- that God's people will be aware of the work of the powers and authorities in society and of their influence in the church.

- that he will unite us and keep us from division.

- for those who have caused division in the body, whether it be intentionally or unintentionally. Pray that they may be graciously accepted and restored.

THE REMAINDER OF THE WEEK

 Questions for Reflection

- In what ways has the dividing work of the powers in society crept into the church? Is it through political ideologies, media conditioning, worldly philosophies, and so forth?

- Have I fully embraced the way of the cross in my own life?

Application

- What is an application that you take away from this section for your faith community?

- What is the personal application that you take away from this section?

Further Study (Optional)

- Read the following article about the new-creation community and the powers and authorities: "A Radically New Humanity: The Function of the *Haustafel* in Ephesians" (etsjets.org).

https://www.etsjets.org/files/JETS-PDFs/48/48-2/48-2-pp317-330_JETS.pdf

1 CORINTHIANS 2:14-3:4

These people were [worldly] because they were still slaves to the desires of the present age. Although they had been baptized and had received the Holy Spirit, they were [worldly] because after baptism they had returned to their old lives, which they had renounced. The Holy Spirit dwells in a person into whom he has poured himself if that person stays firm in the conviction of his new birth.

—Ambrosiaster, 4th century AD

READ

—Read 1 Corinthians 2:14–3:4 out loud at least once.
—Read 1 Corinthians 2:14–3:4 at least once silently to yourself. Read it very slowly, allowing time for each word and phrase to resonate.

REFLECT

A Thought of Reflection

1 Corinthians is often utilized by modern preachers as an example of a messed-up church. This helps emphasize that even though our churches today have many issues, we are no worse off than these early Christians. Despite all their obvious sin and shortcomings, Paul still refers to them as sanctified and holy people (1 Corinthians 1:2). What might shock us, though, is that if we read this letter carefully it becomes obvious that they didn't view themselves as a mess. They thought they were doing well. They believed themselves to be quite spiritual and were proud of that. But how could they be so flawed and yet blind to it? It is easier than we might want to believe.

Paul's point here is that the wisdom of God would result in a church community that is ordered by the equalizing power of the cross. It would be a church that actively sought to tear down the dividing walls of hostility and would not tolerate social hierarchies and advantages created by the sin of the world, namely the lie of status superiority. The person led by the wisdom of the Spirit simply would not tolerate such opposition to true image bearing. Yet, by embracing cultural values like splitting into factions over which teacher they preferred or who brought more honor to their followers, the Corinthian Christians were expressly rejecting God's wisdom and accepting mere human judgments. They were illustrating that they did not have the mind of Christ. Because of this, Paul could not teach them the true depth and unifying power of the cross because they had twisted the gospel by reinterpreting it according to the values of their culture.

This is a mistake that is incredibly easy to make because we need to do nothing in order for it to happen. One of the most pernicious aspects of the various versions of the lie of superiority is that they become baked into the pie of societal structure and then we quickly become desensitized to them. These divisions and privileges for some start to seem normal, and we grow accustomed to inequities as though this is just the way the world is. And it is—when the prevailing wisdom comes from the powers and authorities. Paul wants them, conversely, to order themselves by God's wisdom. He wants them to truly act spiritually as people of the new creation rather than as mere humans of the present age.

Preparation for Reflection

1. Paul challenges the saints in Corinth to be discerning in everything they think, everything they do, everything they believe, and everything they take part in, according to the wisdom of the Spirit. Why do you think they failed to do that?

2. Why do you think Paul was so concerned about something so seemingly trivial as identifying with one teacher over another?

3. According to Severian of Gabala, a late fourth-century preacher in Constantinople, the milk that the Corinthians were stuck on was the moral teaching and blessings of Christianity. They failed to work through the aspects

of the gospel that called them to radically reorder the way their culture and society had been constructed. Do you believe that churches today often make that same mistake? Why or why not?

RECITE

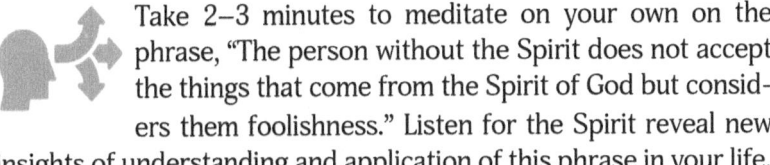

Take 2–3 minutes to meditate on your own on the phrase, "The person without the Spirit does not accept the things that come from the Spirit of God but considers them foolishness." Listen for the Spirit reveal new insights of understanding and application of this phrase in your life.

RESPOND

As you move into a time of prayer, focus on the things you normally pray for but today take some time to pray:

- that the church will be willing to engage in some of the more challenging implications of the gospel of Christ.

- that the church will desire to move past spiritual milk and on to full maturity.

- that we will more and more seek and receive the mind of Christ in all matters.

THE REMAINDER OF THE WEEK

Questions for Reflection

- Are there any of the more difficult aspects of our world that you have avoided and not made subject to God's wisdom?

- Paul says that the fighting and divisions were evidence of their immaturity. Do you see any similar evidence in your church? If so, what can you do to help that situation?

Application

- What is an application that you take away from this section for your faith community?

- What is the personal application that you take away from this section?

Further Study (Optional)

- Read the following article about social status in the Roman world: Ancient History: "Social Pecking Order in the Roman World" (BBC History).

https://www.bbc.co.uk/history/ancient/romans/social_structure_01.shtml

The building does not belong to the workman but the master. If you are building, you must not be split in two, since then the building will collapse. If you are a farm, you must not be divided but rather surrounded by a single fence, the fence of unanimity.
                              —Chrysostom, 4th century AD

READ

—Read 1 Corinthians 3:5–17 out loud at least once.
—Read 1 Corinthians 3:5–17 at least once silently to yourself. Read it very slowly, allowing time for each word and phrase to resonate.

REFLECT

A Thought of Reflection

Paul's concern for the Corinthians in this section is not that it is wrong for them to have teachers and preachers that they prefer or learn more from. Nor does he randomly switch topics from teachers to a diatribe on church-building. The threat is a church that has mimicked the wisdom of the world and remained completely blind to it. This wisdom is in direct opposition to the heart of the gospel. To gain honor and status by following certain teachers and then split into factional arguments over which teacher brings the most prestige is precisely what the culture around them did as the regular course of events. It was the accepted norm, not a new creation.

Rather than being exalted masters and leaders, Paul and Apollos were just lowly servants. Status and superiority simply have no place in God's kingdom. And just as they were blind to their cultural influences, so we can remain unaware of how we have been conditioned to think politically by our favorite news source, operate with a philosophy of our identity that comes from the wisdom of this age, or remain blind to the impact of segregation and injustice created by our versions of the lie of superiority such as that which has resulted in ongoing inequities in our society.

The only foundation we can wisely and rightly build on is the crucified and resurrected Jesus Christ. For us, that means following the way of the cross that leads to a new life. Paul does not mince words here. To build the wisdom of the culture around us into the life of the church is work that destroys the temple that God created by bringing together the social elite and the non-elite. The world cannot maintain this type of radical diversity because it does not have the foundation that can hold it. Only in Christ can this be built and maintained as the manifold wisdom of God is displayed to the powers and authorities and the rest of the world through the church (Ephesians 3:10).

Preparation for Reflection

1. What point is Paul making when he says that he planted the seed and Apollos watered it, but God makes it grow?

2. Why is it important to understand that Paul is not just speaking of theoretical doctrine here but is concerned with how they live with, think about, and treat one another in the body of Christ?

3. It might be easy to look at a passage like this and quickly become judgmental toward others. How do humility and the principles from Matthew 7:1–6 help guide us in this instance?

RECITE

Take 2–3 minutes to meditate on the phrase, "God's temple is sacred, and you together are that temple." Listen to the Spirit reveal new insights of understanding and application of this phrase in your life..

RESPOND

As you move into a time of prayer, focus on the things you normally pray for but today take some time to pray:

- that the church will carefully examine the effects of influence from the culture around you, building only on the foundation of Christ.

- that each member will humbly and earnestly examine themselves to see if they have allowed cultural influences to impact their view of the gospel and how Christians should live.

- that God will lead you into humility and grant you wisdom and discernment in these areas.

THE REMAINDER OF THE WEEK

 Questions for Reflection

- Have I accepted some ways of viewing the world or thinking about others that are the result of worldly influence rather than being the fruit of the gospel?

- What can I do to help build up and bring unity to God's temple?

Application

- What is an application that you take away from this section for your faith community?

- What is the personal application that you take away from this section?

Further Study (Optional)

- Read the following article about Paul's meaning in 1 Cor. 3:10–15 and its connection with the book of 1 Enoch Ronald Herms, "'Being Saved without Honor': A Conceptual Link between 1 Corinthians 3 and 1 Enoch 50?" PDF (Academia.edu).

https://www.academia.edu/2972204/_Being_Saved_without_Honor_A_Conceptual_Link_between_1_Corinthians_3_and_1Enoch_50

1 CORINTHIANS 3:18–4:5

Paul accuses the Corinthians of two things. First, they exaggerate their praise, and second, they condemn others when they have no right to judge.
> —Theodoret of Cyrus, 5th century AD

READ

—Read 1 Corinthians 3:18–4:5 out loud at least once.
—Read 1 Corinthians 3:18–4:5 at least once silently to yourself. Read it very slowly, allowing time for each word and phrase to resonate.

REFLECT

A Thought of Reflection

Discipling is an ongoing formative endeavor that forms our thinking and ultimately our behavior into a certain pattern or shape. True spiritual discipling methodically forms us into the shape and character of Christ. But if we do not intentionally choose to be transformed by such discipling (Romans 12:2), we will be conformed to the pattern of the world (Romans 12:2). This is no accident. The powers and authorities are constantly seeking through culture, media, societal norms, and many other means to antidisciple us. Since we are surrounded by antidiscipling (counterfeit discipling), it happens almost automatically unless we consciously reject and counteract it. Otherwise, we remain largely ignorant of its effects and will often blend tenets of antidiscipling with our life in Christ. This is exactly what the believers in Corinth had done.

This is such an important commonality in much of what Paul is trying to teach the church in this letter that he spends more space on dealing with their divisions over teachers than just about any other topic in the letter. It is not that this issue is more vital than the others Paul will approach; rather, he is using it as the opening salvo to teach them the basic principle that they have fallen victim to. They have remained blind to the influence and ongoing effects of the world's wisdom and systems and have let them shape their lives in Christ. When they established their status by boasting about which teacher they identified with, they were doing much more than that. They were indiscriminately accepting the so-called wisdom—in other words, the behavior and standards—of their culture. But even more than that. When they did this, they rejected the wisdom of God by not living according to the values of the new creation. There are no hierarchies, advantages, or inequities in a community of image-bearers.

One of the problems with the lie of superiority is that it implements limited human judgment by determining that the worth or value of some is greater than that of others. Which teacher was of higher status and thus more valuable? Which social class is more valuable? Which nation is more valuable? Which political party is more valuable? Which race is more valuable? Which gender is more valuable? The moment we assign or accept primary identities other than that of image-bearer is the instant that we begin to judge and assign value. That does not mean that there aren't realities in life that we must be aware of and face because of these secondary identities, but our primary identity and that of others must always be as a beloved image-bearer. That is the wisdom of God.

Preparation for Reflection

1. Why is it important to comprehend that your primary identity before God is that of a beloved image-bearer?

2. What are the dangers of identifying, labeling, and treating others by secondary identities as though that were their primary identity?

3. Why does Paul adamantly refuse to judge the value, worth, or status of a human being?

RECITE

Take 2–3 minutes to meditate on your own on the phrase, "Judge nothing before the appointed time." Listen for the Spirit to reveal new insights of understanding and application of this phrase in your life.

RESPOND

As you move into a time of prayer, focus on the things you normally pray for but today take some time to pray:

- that each member of your fellowship will have the courage to take an honest look at themselves to see if they have let the wisdom of the world dictate some of their thoughts and behaviors.

- that God will inspire us to view and treat all other humans as beloved image-bearers.

- that this church will become a place free of judging the worth and value of others, whether it be by intentional action or through passively accepting the values of the world.

THE REMAINDER OF THE WEEK

Questions for Reflection

- What are ways that I subtly or not-so-subtly label and categorize people according to identities other than image-bearer?

- Do I need to address judging or assigning value to others?

Application

- What is an application that you take away from this section for your faith community?

- What is the personal application that you take away from this section?

Further Study (Optional)

- Read the following article about honor and identity in Rome: (4) Nick Galasso, "Honor and the Performance of Roman State Identity" (Academia.edu).

https://www.academia.edu/3846206/Honor_and_The_Performance_of_Roman_State_Identity

1 CORINTHIANS 4:6-21

Not speaking against sins would have been impossible since they would have remained uncorrected. To have left the wound untended after having spoken would have been harsh. Therefore, Paul apologizes for being severe, because so far from destroying the effect of the knife it makes it sink in even deeper, while at the same time it looks toward soothing the pain of the wound. When a person is told that these things are being said in love and not in reproach, he will be more open to receiving correction.

—Chrysostom, 4th century AD

READ

—Read 1 Corinthians 4:6–21 out loud at least once.
—Read 1 Corinthians 4:6–21 at least once silently to yourself. Read it very slowly, allowing time for each word and phrase to resonate.

REFLECT

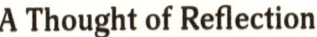

A Thought of Reflection

One of the primary problems of the world's wisdom is that it cannot deliver on what it promises. It offers success, happiness, victory, unity, and a host of other positive outcomes. But in the end, it delivers these only for some, and only partially at that, or it does not deliver them at all. Rather than success, we often find idolatry. Promised happiness ends in the constant need for more. What is a victory for some is a terrible defeat for others. The promise of unity breaks down into an elusive and never-attainable dream. And on it goes.

The Corinthians believed they could mix their faith and the wisdom of God with aspects of their cultural norms. This was probably not intentional. It happened because they failed to discern the impact of the influence of their culture and had not fully thought through all the implications of the gospel. They missed all that and thought they were fine. They thought they were already living out the rule and reign of the kingdom for the world to see. They thought they could be disciples of Jesus and still care about status advancement and the advantages of the elite, boasting to establish their right to do anything they wanted, which was the privilege of the socially strong.

The problem was obvious to Paul: They were taking the shape of the society around them rather than the shape of the cross. And the shape of the cross is the only form that God's people are to embrace. Most Christians would confess that they want nothing more than to live out the way of the cross, but saying it is one thing and doing it is another. We want to reign. We desire to be admired and thought of as wise. We like privileges. We want a blessing. But we don't tend to want the type of blessing that Paul and Jesus received—the blessing of laying down everything and carrying nothing but the cross. We reject a life that spurns our rights, advantages, and privileges for the sake of others, especially the most vulnerable. We squeal in protest if we are slighted in the least or are ridiculed or marginalized as followers of Jesus. We don't like to be cross shaped any more than the Corinthians did. And we might be just as blind to our true condition as they were.

Preparation for Reflection

1. Why do you think Paul decided to use sarcasm here to make his point about the Corinthian church?

2. What are some specific ways that you see the modern church preferring the comforts and privilege of culture or the status of our economic situation, our citizenship, or something similar, rather than being a cross-shaped people?

3. Considering the context of this letter and his statements in this passage, what does Paul mean when he says that "the kingdom of God is not a matter of talk but of power"?

RECITE

Take 2–3 minutes to meditate on your own on the phrase, "When we are cursed, we bless; when we are persecuted, we endure it; when we are slandered, we answer kindly." Listen for the Spirit to reveal things about the meaning and application of this phrase in your life.

RESPOND

As you move into a time of prayer, focus on the things you normally pray for but today take some time to pray:

- for humility for yourself and others.

- thanking God for all that he has done to help the church escape enslavement to the present age and the darkness of the powers and authorities.

- that God will continue to help your fellowship see the areas where it needs to grow and become more cross shaped.

THE REMAINDER OF THE WEEK

Questions for Reflection

- Do I pursue comfort, status, and privilege more than the way of the cross?

- What can I do today to put the interests of someone in need ahead of my own?

Application

- What is an application that you take away from this section for your faith community?

- What is the personal application for yourself?

Further Study (Optional)

- Read this article about sarcasm in the Bible: "The Bible's Use of Sarcasm, Irony, and Denunciation" (christianstudylibrary.org).ademia.edu).

https://www.christianstudylibrary.org/article/bible's-use-sarcasm-irony-and-denunciation

1 CORINTHIANS 5:1-13

Paul says that the Corinthians are to blame because by taking pride in this man they have hindered him from repenting. Here he indicates that the problem is one for the whole church, not just for an individual. This is why he uses the symbol of the leaven, which, although a small thing in itself, transforms the whole lump into its nature.

—Chrysostom, 4th century AD

READ

—Read 1 Corinthians 5:1–13 out loud at least once.
—Read 1 Corinthians 5:1–13 at least once silently to yourself. Read it very slowly, allowing time for each word and phrase to resonate.

REFLECT

A Thought of Reflection

This situation seems puzzling until we understand the context behind it a little better. A young man was sleeping with his stepmother. This was against Roman law... unless you were of elite social status. Then, custom dictated that the behavior be overlooked because, for the noble, all things were permissible. It appears that a wealthy patron of some reputation had become a Christian, and they spent more energy reveling in his status and increasing their status a bit by association with him than they did on calling this man to the repentant life of the new creation. This is a case of his individual sin being obfuscated by the systemic and cultural sin of social superiority. The congregation failed to see either category of sin because they were still operating by their cultural wisdom and perspectives.

By allowing the effects of the lie of superiority into the church, they were not only harming this man, but they were also subjecting all the saints to the injustice of privilege and disadvantage. They were operating by the values of the realm of Satan sown by the powers and authorities and rooted deeply in the social systems and structures in which they were living and operating. For this reason, Paul demands that they turn the man over to Satan. If he wants to live by the values of the present, evil age, then he should not have the cover of the church. This would only harm him by fooling him into believing he is part of the new creation. This was vital for the church as well. Just a little bit of the world's values allowed and accepted into their collective lives would quickly affect the entire ethos and life of the congregation.

Paul knows that if they allow the smallest morsel of the lie of superiority into their midst, they will quickly fail to be a sample of the new creation. They will no longer be witnesses to a world enslaved by the powers. He doesn't want them to recoil and completely withdraw from the world; quite the opposite. He wants them to be the community of image-bearers they were called to be so that they might invite the world into a whole new way of being human, one where superiority and hierarchy are actively exposed and erased and the only thing that remains is the way of the cross.

Preparation for Reflection

1. With the historical and cultural context of this situation in mind, what might a contemporary example of a similar situation look like? What can we learn from Paul's ferocity and clarity in dealing with this overlooking of personal sin and the resulting inequity of systemic sin?

2. Why is it important to note that when Paul says, "A little yeast leavens the whole batch of dough," the yeast to which he refers is their embracing of worldly wisdom rather than the man himself?

3. Why does Paul insert his thought about keeping the festival of Passover and the sacrificed Christ? What is his point in including that in this situation?

RECITE

Take 2–3 minutes to meditate on the phrase, "A little yeast leavens the whole batch of dough." Listen for the Spirit to reveal new insights of understanding and application of this phrase in your life.

RESPOND

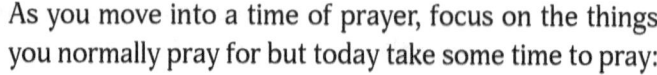

As you move into a time of prayer, focus on the things you normally pray for but today take some time to pray:

- that the Holy Spirit will move the church to awaken to any instances of seeing the kingdom through worldly lenses rather than seeing the world through a kingdom lens.

- that God will allow us to be clear examples of the new creation to a watching world.

- that God will help you to respond to passages like these humbly and with a heart for self-examination rather than jumping to the judgment of others.

THE REMAINDER OF THE WEEK

 Questions for Reflection

- Do I tolerate historical and cultural advantages and inequities taking root in my heart or in the life of the church?

- If the only sample of the new creation someone ever experienced was my life, what would they be getting?

Application

- What is an application that you take away from this section for your faith community?

- What is the personal application that you take away from this section?

Further Study (Optional)

- Read the following article about civic identity in Rome and the Corinthian church: "The role of civic identity on the Pauline mission in Corinth," (bethel.edu).

https://www.academia.edu/2862018/The_role_of_civic_identity_on_the_Pauline_mission_in_Corinth

The kingdom of God must be purified of all sin and immorality, so that God may reign in it.

—Origen, 3rd century AD

READ

—Read 1 Corinthians 6:1–11 out loud at least once.

—Read 1 Corinthians 6:1–11 at least once silently to yourself. Read it very slowly, allowing time for each word and phrase to resonate.

REFLECT

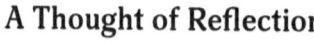

A Thought of Reflection

United States civil courts are designed to bring about justice, first and foremost. It might be difficult for us to grasp, but blind justice was not the primary function of the Roman civil courts. They were heavily tilted toward those of wealth and high status. Those who were poor and of low status did not have the same access and privilege in the courts. In fact, in most circumstances, the non-elites could not sue the elites. It could be argued that the primary function of Roman civil courts was to maintain the social order and the privilege of the nobles rather than to mete out justice fairly. The courts exacerbated and protected the inequities of the social system based on the lie of superiority.

At the same time, Roman custom and culture dictated that family members were one group of people that you would not bring civil charges against. It was better to allow oneself to be ripped off than to press a case against a family member.

Both social realities presented a problem for Paul when he was informed that some Christians were taking others to court. The first problem was that these were undoubtedly cases of elite Christians suing non-elites. Those who were to be part of the new-creation community were now being subjected to the same systemic injustices they faced in the world. The second problem was that these lawsuits sent a clear message to the rest of the Roman world that the Christians didn't act like family members despite their claims to be a new family created by the blood of Christ.

By rejecting the benefits of family and subjecting weaker members to the social inequities and division of the powers and authorities that were intertwined with the Roman system, the disciples in Corinth were abandoning their call to model the new creation and be an advance sample of the age to come when they would partner with God to exercise his reign over all parts of creation. For Paul, failing to exhibit the justice of God as a community was akin to idolatry, adultery, thievery, and other non-kingdom behaviors. The problem was that some were more concerned with their rights than with loving their brothers and sisters. And it is to that destructive reality that Paul will turn his full attention next.

Preparation for Reflection

1. Why do you think Paul was so concerned about matters of justice, equality, and social issues that, on the surface, seem unrelated to strictly spiritual matters?

2. How do you think the non-elites in the Corinthian congregation felt when they first heard Paul's directives in this passage? What signal did Paul's implementation of the gospel in a situation like this send to them?

3. Why do you think it never occurred to the Corinthians that wealthy elites taking socially weaker members to court to exercise their rights and privileges instead of resolving these issues within the church body was fundamentally opposed to the values of the kingdom of God?

RECITE

Take 2–3 minutes to meditate on your own on the phrase, "Why not rather be wronged?" Listen for the Spirit to reveal new things about the meaning and application of this phrase to your life.

RESPOND

As you move into a time of prayer, focus on the things you normally pray for but today take some time to pray:

- for all that have been treated unjustly by the social structures and systems of the world.

- that the Holy Spirit will help your church community be discerning and creative in recognizing the systems of the world that perpetuate injustice and, as much as possible, become a haven from them.

- to be ever more aware of cleansing, sanctifying, and justifying grace.

THE REMAINDER OF THE WEEK

Questions for Reflection

- Have I ever considered or asked other members of our fellowship if the church has unintentionally or otherwise allowed members to continue to be affected by unjust systems of the world within the life of the body?

- What can I do to be more aware of the needs of disciples who might be less fortunate than I am?

Application

- What is an application that you take away from this section for your faith community?

- What is the personal application that you take away from this section?

Further Study (Optional)

- Read the following article about the cultural background of 1 Corinthians 6: "Brother against Brother: *Controversiae* about Inheritance Disputes and 1 Corinthians 6:1–11" (JSTOR).

https://www.jstor.org/stable/10.15699/jbibllite.133.1.179

1 CORINTHIANS 6:12-20

DAY 11

You are all members of Christ because you have united to him by being born again of the Spirit. You have the hope that you will rise again, just as he rose.

—Theodore of Mopsuestia, 5th century AD

READ

—Read 1 Corinthians 6:12–20 out loud at least once.
—Read 1 Corinthians 6:12–20 at least once silently to yourself. Read it very slowly, allowing time for each word and phrase to resonate.

REFLECT

A Thought of Reflection

When elite Corinthian males reached the age of 18, they received the *toga virilis*, which indicated that they were men and now had full rights to participate in the gluttony, drunkenness, and after-dinner promiscuity (often with prostitutes who were brought in) of the banquets that were common celebrations. They believed that this enjoyment of life was what nature (often interchangeable with God or the gods in their mind) intended. None of this was seen as wrong in the Greco-Roman culture. For young men, especially the elite who had come of age, they had the right to do anything. To put it another way, "Everything is permissible."

What seems to have been taking place is that those disciples who were higher up on the social scale in Corinth saw it as their right to take part in the many banquets and celebrations that were part of normal life. Much like a US citizen who might justify the exercise of their rights by citing the Bill of Rights or American freedoms and customs, these Corinthian Christians were citing the slogan of the Corinthian elites, "I have the right to do anything," as well as the Greco-Roman conventions that the stomach and body were designed for pleasure and were separate issues from one's soul.

The element they were missing is that everything is spiritual. Whether they exercised their freedoms and rights or not was an issue of the new creation. What they did with their time, resources, and yes, their bodies too, were matters of the new creation. Paul's underlying point that he will expound upon in the coming chapters is that our rights are not the ground from which a Christian should start. When we understand that we were bought at the cross and have been called to live the way of the cross, we will fully grasp that this changes everything.

Preparation for Reflection

1. "I have the right to do anything" was a common slogan among Corinthian elites. Can you think of similar sayings or sentiments that Christians in the USA might use to order their thinking or justify certain behaviors?

2. The Corinthians had never grasped that their culture had led them to move the way they approached treating others, their rights, and even their approach to food, drink, and sexual pleasure at banquets outside the realm of spiritual significance. Are there any areas that our culture encourages us to leave outside the realm of our spirituality?

3. Why does Paul allude to the resurrection of Christ and to our future resurrection? How does that help establish his point?

RECITE

 Take 2–3 minutes to meditate on the phrase, "A little yeast leavens the whole batch of dough." Listen for the Spirit to reveal new insights of understanding and application of this phrase to your life.

RESPOND

As you move into a time of prayer, focus on the things you normally pray for but today take some time to pray:

- that God will help you understand the impact of the future resurrection of believers on our present actions.

- that God will help you to see things that you can do that will be beneficial to the body and help build it up.

- for growing awareness of how our culture can work to subtly lead us away from the way of the cross and accept things as valid that are completely opposed to the image-bearing life.

THE REMAINDER OF THE WEEK

Questions for Reflection

- Are there times when I have exercised my rights or preferences at the expense of others in the body?

- Are there areas of my life in which I have been affected by my society and culture that I have not addressed?

Application

- What is an application that you take away from this section for your faith community?

- What is the personal application that you take away from this section?

Further Study (Optional)

- Read the following article about 1 Corinthians 6:12–20: "Gluttons and Drunks in the Church – 1 Corinthians 6:12–20" (readingacts.com).

https://readingacts.com/2019/10/07/1-corinthians-612-20-gluttons-and-drunks-in-the-church/

You have given up your wife, to whom you are bound. This is a big step you have taken. You are not abusing her, you say, but claiming that you can be chaste and live more purely. But look how your poor wife is being destroyed as a result, because she is unable to endure your purity! You should sleep with your wife, not for your sake but for hers.

—Theodore of Mopsuestia, 5th century AD

READ

—Read 1 Corinthians 7:1–7 out loud at least once.

—Read 1 Corinthians 7:1–7 at least once silently to yourself. Read it very slowly, allowing time for each word and phrase to resonate.

REFLECT

A Thought of Reflection

Scattered throughout this letter are responses from Paul to either a topic in the Corinthian church that he sees needs addressing or instances where they ask him questions and he responds. In both situations, he peppers his thoughts with quotations or slogans from the Corinthians to which he then responds with corrective teaching. We see an example of that in this passage as Paul utilizes their question about marriage and the thought that at least some in the church were expressing, "It is good for a man not to have sexual relations with a woman." This offers the perfect opportunity for the apostle to illustrate an important point in his ongoing discussion about the role of rights for the disciples of Jesus.

It seems that some in Corinth were denouncing sexual relations in marriage to develop an ongoing discipline of prayer in response to the crisis they were facing, likely a severe famine and series of earthquakes in the area. For Paul, this is an illustration of exercising one's preference or even devotion that was self-focused rather than being others-focused. It was to put one's rights ahead of what was beneficial or constructive.

We should not miss how countercultural his instructions were in a first-century context. To affirm that a woman did not have complete authority over her own body was standard. But to assert that, in the same way, a husband did not have authority over his own body and that neither spouse should exert their rights or will over the other was downright revolutionary. If they did desire to focus on a special season of prayer and felt that temporary abstinence was helpful, it should be a mutual decision as equal partners. The bottom line is that the way of the cross extends to every aspect of the life of a disciple. Even in a foundational relationship like marriage, the surrounding culture does not determine our behavior. Only the cross does that.

Preparation for Reflection

1. What do you think the Corinthian believers were missing about discipleship that left them so vulnerable to their cultural influence and so prone to missing the way of the cross?

2. What specific challenges were there for a typical Corinthian husband that are implied in Paul's call for mutual submission, respect, and belonging?

3. When was the last time your fellowship collectively considered how the way of the cross would impact and challenge every aspect of your life and behaviors? What are the potential advantages of doing so? Are there any disadvantages?

RECITE

Take 2–3 minutes to meditate on your own on the phrase, "In the same way, the husband does not have authority over his own body but yields it to his wife." Listen for the Spirit to reveal new insights of understanding and application of this phrase to your life.

RESPOND

As you move into a time of prayer, focus on the things you normally pray for but today take some time to pray:

- for strong and mutually respectful marriages in your fellowship.

- that both husbands and wives in your church will have healthy marriages that strive to put the needs of one another ahead of their rights and preferences.

- specifically for any marriages that you know are struggling and need grace and growth.

THE REMAINDER OF THE WEEK

Questions for Reflection

- Do I strive to consider others and put what is beneficial to the body ahead of my interests whenever possible and appropriate?

- If I am married or single, do I view it as a gift from God?

Application

- What is an application that you take away from this section for your faith community?

- What is the personal application that you take away from this section?

Further Study (Optional)

- Read the following article about marriage in the Roman cultural world: "Marriage and love life in ancient Rome" (imperiumromanum.pl).

https://imperiumromanum.pl/en/roman-society/marriage-and-love-life-in-ancient-rome/

1 CORINTHIANS 7:8-16

DAY 13

Separations are best avoided if at all possible, but if not, the wife should not take another husband.

—Chrysostom, 4th century AD

READ

—Read 1 Corinthians 7:8–16 out loud at least once.
—Read 1 Corinthians 7:8–16 at least once silently to yourself. Read it very slowly, allowing time for each word and phrase to resonate.

REFLECT

A Thought of Reflection

In the world of first-century Rome, divorce was common and easy, especially for the elite and those of high status. The moment a spouse was no longer happy, they could dissolve the marriage by simply declaring so and moving on. There was great societal pressure to quickly get remarried. It was so common to leave one marriage for another that Romans often joked that you could tell how old someone was to the year by counting how many ex-spouses they had. It was the ultimate exaltation of their pleasures and rights above everything else. Paul shows how this is turned on its head in the new creation and provides wisdom and guidance for three specific situations: those who were once married but no longer are, those who are married, and those who share a marriage with an unbeliever.

One note of caution: We must navigate passages like this carefully for two reasons. The first is that Paul is operating in common-law society and culture, while we come from a statutory society and culture. That means we view instructions in a black-and-white way. We follow the letter of the law. Common-law cultures valued principles, wisdom, and guidance. They didn't view instructions as strict rules but rather as general wisdom to be applied wisely to each case. This can lead to us reading writings from common-law cultures too narrowly or restrictively. The second reason is that Paul wrote to deal with very specific cultural situations that don't always directly translate to our own without a great deal of discernment and thought.

Paul's guidance to the widows and widowers is that it is an honorable choice to remain unmarried and focus on the kingdom. Society need not pressure them to rush into a marriage, but if it proves too much temptation, then it is also honorable to marry again. To the married, he guides them to reject the easy divorce and exaltation of personal rights in the culture around them and remain married if at all possible. Yet if a spouse does separate, they are not excluded from the body but counseled to not remarry again. And to those who might feel pressure to divorce their unbelieving spouse, Paul flips the fear that they will be made profane by such a union. The influence of new creation on their family will have the opposite effect. It will make their family "holy," which in this instance, likely means that it will make them different from other families. They will influence their family toward good rather than the family making them unclean.

Preparation for Reflection

1. Why do you think it is important to understand that the New Testament letters were much more intended to be guides leading people toward wisdom to be applied in difficult situations than rules to simply be implemented with little or no thought?

2. Do you think that contemporary Christianity gives equal honor and position to those who choose to get married and those who choose to remain unmarried? If not, what do you think the church can do to address that situation carefully and spiritually?

3. Why do you think Paul clarifies some of his comments with the qualifier, "I, not the Lord?" Do you think he intended to signal that this was merely his opinion that could be accepted or rejected equally? Or was he clarifying between a specific command from Jesus and apos-

tolic wisdom that was to be discerned and implemented? Or do you think he had other intentions?

RECITE

Take 2–3 minutes to meditate on your own on the phrase, "God has called us to live in peace." Listen for the Spirit to reveal new insights of understanding and application of this phrase to your life.

RESPOND

As you move into a time of prayer, focus on the things you normally pray for but today take some time to pray:

- that the marriages in your congregation will be strong and continue to grow in their Christlikeness.

- that those who choose to remain unmarried will feel valued and loved by the rest of the church and find ways to fully participate in and contribute to the life of the body.

- for those who have spouses who are not currently following Jesus. Pray that they will be refreshed and strengthened to continue to show the love of Christ to their spouse and that it will have a lasting effect on their family.

THE REMAINDER OF THE WEEK

Questions for Reflection

- Do I treat the married and unmarried with equal levels of respect and inclusion?

- How can I encourage those who are in a different marriage situation than I am?

Application

- What is an application that you take away from this section for your faith community?

- What is the personal application that you take away from this section?

Further Study (Optional)

- Read the following article about Paul's view of remarriage: Carly Daniel-Hughes, "Only in the Lord: Debates over Paul's View of Remarriage in Early Christianity," PDF (Academia.edu).

https://www.academia.edu/en/26898181/Only_in_the_Lord_Debates_over_Pauls_View_of_Remarriage_in_Early_Christianity_pdf

1 CORINTHIANS 7:17-24
DAY 14

Paul wants to show that slave and master are equal. We are all freedmen of Christ because he has set us free from the tyranny of Satan, and we are voluntary slaves of Christ because, having set us free, he led us into his kingdom.
—Oecumenius, 6th century AD

READ

—Read 1 Corinthians 7:17–24 out loud at least once.
—Read 1 Corinthians 7:17–24 at least once silently to yourself. Read it very slowly, allowing time for each word and phrase to resonate.

REFLECT

A Thought of Reflection

Paul seems to have had at least two purposes that run parallel to one another in this letter. He was answering some of the questions and concerns that the Corinthians had expressed in their correspondence with him. And he wants to challenge them in the areas in which they had allowed the unjust elements of the culture around them into the life of the church. That included stubborn blindness to the acceptance of certain status and social superiority categories. Some in Corinth believed that it was a superior state to be single or celibate rather than married. In this chapter, Paul seeks to demonstrate the un-gospel reality of that mindset. Although he has his preferences, he will not allow a mindset that one is better or godlier than the other. Being single is not superior to being married. Both are a gift.

To illustrate this truth, Paul brings out two very relevant examples of other areas where there were temptations to exalt superiority of position or status. Paul rejects ethnic superiority between the circumcised Jews and the uncircumcised Gentiles as well as the status of slave or free. This was not a case of Paul calling them to be blind to their differences and pretend they did not exist, effectively locking the disadvantaged into their position. His point is that they are the new-creation people. They are creating an alternate community and reality where there are no advantages to these identities. They need not be obsessed with social climbing or gaining a higher status like the people around them. If they were of lower status like slaves, that need not trouble them in the body of Christ if it was operating as it should. Of course, it had not been, which is why Paul is so direct and confrontational in this letter. Yet Paul does not slip into naivete either. They still experience the realities of being in lower-status groups in the world, so he does qualify his comments. No, they don't need to status climb in the body of Christ, but if they can become free, then by all means they should.

Paul strikes a tension when it comes to our identities and statuses that requires a great deal of discernment. In the alternate community of the new creation, there should be no hierarchies, special privileges, or status levels. None of those identity markers is superior to any other. If the disciples are living justly, they need not worry about their status in the body of Christ. Yet the reality is that they will still face injustice and negative treatment based on those identities in the present age and should not simply resign themselves to lower status as though God wants them in that position. At every turn, what matters is demonstrating the life of the new creation. That takes wisdom, intentionality, humility, and creativity.

Preparation for Reflection

1. Why do you think Paul was so thorough in going through all the areas in which the Corinthians were mimicking the wisdom of the world?

2. How do you think Paul's words here would have been received by those of lower status? What would have been the challenges for those of higher status in reading this letter?

3. What is so important about the qualifier that Paul tells the believers that were enslaved: that if they could gain their freedom, they should do so?

RECITE

Take 2–3 minutes to meditate on the phrase, "You were bought at a price; do not become slaves of human beings." Listen for the Spirit to reveal new insights of understanding and application of this phrase to your life.

RESPOND

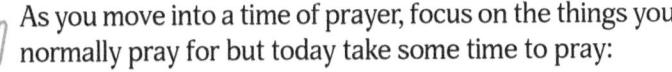

As you move into a time of prayer, focus on the things you normally pray for but today take some time to pray:

- for those in your church that are socially or economically disadvantaged.

- for the church to wipe out the advantages and disadvantages of status and position in the life of the body.

- for wisdom for your church community as you continue to work out the realities of being the new-creation people.

THE REMAINDER OF THE WEEK

Questions for Reflection

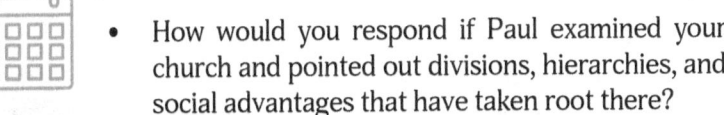

- How would you respond if Paul examined your church and pointed out divisions, hierarchies, and social advantages that have taken root there?

- Is there anything you can do that you haven't done to this point to help the new-creation life flourish in your church?

Application

- How will you apply this to your faith community?
- How will you personally apply this section?

Further Study (Optional)

- Read the following article about Paul's view of identity in the world and Christ: Laura Hunt, "Paul's Rule in 1 Corinthians 7:17–24: Contemporary Limitations and Challenges for Existing Identities in Christ," PDF (Academia.edu).

https://www.academia.edu/41287946/Pauls_Rule_in_1_Corinthians_7_17_24_Contemporary_Limitations_and_Challenges_for_Existing_Identities_in_Christ

1 CORINTHIANS 7:25-40

Some rules are given as commandments of God, while others are more flexible and left by God to the decision of the individual. The first kind is those commandments that pertain to salvation. The others are better because even if we do not keep them, we shall still be saved. There is no merit in doing what is obligatory, but there is in doing that which is optional.

—Ambrosiaster, 4th century AD

READ

—Read 1 Corinthians 7:25–40 out loud at least once.
—Read 1 Corinthians 7:25–40 at least once silently to yourself. Read it very slowly, allowing time for each word and phrase to resonate.

REFLECT

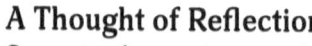

A Thought of Reflection

Some in the ancient world argued that it was better to be married and that remaining single relegated someone to an inferior status. At the same time, other traditions argued that singlehood and celibacy were superior because they avoided distractions and the comfort of marriage.

To gain a full appreciation for the opinions Paul shares with the Corinthians here, there are some things that we must understand about the ancient world that are different from our own. He wants them to appreciate the need to avoid whatever might distract them from embracing and living out the gospel in their cultural context. Getting married in the Roman world carried a bevy of serious social responsibilities to the extended family and as a citizen, householder, and political participant in the social square. Marriage exalted someone in their public status, but there were major strings attached that simply do not apply today.

Paul strikes a balance, honoring both choices and denoting

neither as universally superior. He does urge them to discern the present situation, which was very likely a severe famine (and possibly an impending war that would destroy the temple in Jerusalem). Those are matters that should be weighed considering the new creation. But in giving freedom, Paul honors both marriage and singleness, which brought especially women into a newfound position of empowerment and mutual status that was not otherwise available.

He even uses hyperbolic end-of-the-world language to stress the relative importance of things concerning the gospel over worldly things, to keep their eyes on the single-minded service of the Lord. Above all, Paul desires for his dear friends to be empowered to serve Christ without distraction or anxiety. There is simply not one status or state that is inherently superior to the other. They have the freedom to choose but should always do so in all wisdom and in light of the new creation.

Preparation for Reflection

1. How does Paul strike a balance here between personal freedoms and the obligation to live out the reality of the gospel in devotion to Christ?

2. Why do you think Paul preferred the state of being single?

3. If Paul said singlehood was the preferred status in their situation, why did he affirm those who wished to get married?

RECITE

Take 2–3 minutes to meditate on the phrase, "I am saying this...that you may live in a right way in undivided devotion to the Lord." Listen for the Spirit to reveal new insights of understanding and application of this phrase to your life.

RESPOND

As you move into a time of prayer, focus on the things you normally pray for but today take some time to pray:

- for those who are single that they may know that

they are honored in the body and be allowed to glorify God to the fullest in their lives.

- for those who are married that they may honor their spouses and together discover in increasing measure how they might glorify God as a family.

- that both singles and marrieds would honor the calling of one another, not be separated from one another in church life, and not emphasize one way of life to the diminishment of the other.

THE REMAINDER OF THE WEEK

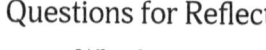 Questions for Reflection

- Whether you are single or married, are you living with full devotion to the Lord?

- Whether you are single or married, how can you encourage those who are living out the other calling?

Application

- What is an application that you take away from this section for your faith community?

- What is the personal application that you take away from this section?

Further Study (Optional)

- Read the following article about the present crisis in Corinth: Bible Gem 378 – "The Present Crisis – What is it? (1 Cor 7:26)" (Berean Insights).

https://www.bereaninsights.org/bible-gem-378-the-present-crisis-what-is-it-1-cor-726/

1 CORINTHIANS 8:1-13

Love builds up. It moves in the realm of truth, not of opinion.
—Clement of Alexandria, 2nd century AD

READ

—Read 1 Corinthians 8:1–13 out loud at least once.
—Read 1 Corinthians 8:1–13 at least once silently to yourself. Read it very slowly, allowing time for each word and phrase to resonate.

REFLECT

A Thought of Reflection

Paul returns directly to the issue of Christians exalting their rights over the needs of others, and the specific issue in Corinth of the high-status members doing so at the expense of their low-status brothers and sisters. What may have seemed like a simple case of some members simply accessing the societal privileges that their status and custom afforded them was, for Paul, another instance of believers reflecting the sin of superiority rather than being an image-bearing community.

There was a clear divide in Corinthian culture between the strong (high-status) and the weak (low-status). Those of high status had advantages of wealth, privilege, and even knowledge. This had carried over into the attitudes of strong-group Christians, who seemed to think that their knowledge had allowed them the insight that idolatry and eating meat at the elite meals they had access to were not connected in any way. The weak didn't possess this "special" and basic knowledge. Eating meat was incredibly expensive, and these types of meals were not something they had to navigate or think about often, if at all. The strong felt their social capital and knowledge gave them religious authority, and this gave them the right to do whatever was not overtly sinful. This thinking turned this economic divide into a religious divide as well, because the weak were scandalized by the idea of their Christian siblings partaking in idolatrous activities. Eating meat in the highbrow temple dining rooms was a normal and proper meal to the strong. It was pure idolatry to the weak, who had no social framework to assume otherwise.

Paul says that this type of knowledge is not rooted in love; it does nothing but puff up. This is a strong reminder for those who think they have greater political, ideological, or historical insight than other believers. The apostle does not call for greater education but status reversal. Simply teaching the weak would allow the strong to get what they want but would change nothing about status superiority. Yes, the strong had greater monotheistic knowledge, but the way of the cross beckons them to give up their privilege and abstain from these meals for the good of the weak. This would disrupt the whole system of status and economic privilege. Paul opts to disrupt and overturn the social order through love. It is the only thing that can truly alleviate the tension between groups and allow them to be harbingers of the new creation.

Preparation for Reflection

1. What are some ways that Paul's statement "Knowledge puffs up while love builds up" could be used out of context by Christians? Why is it important to understand passages like this in their context?

2. Why do you think Paul was so concerned about all these issues surrounding their social status and how they behaved in their "private" lives?

3. What are the implications of being a community that values love over the exercise of one's rights?

RECITE

 Take 2–3 minutes to meditate on your own on the phrase, "Be careful, however, that the exercise of your rights does not become a stumbling block to the weak." Listen for the Spirit to reveal new insights of understanding and application of this phrase to your life.

RESPOND

As you move into a time of prayer, focus on the things you normally pray for but today take some time to pray:

- for unity among God's people, especially across lines that easily divide people in the world and that have the potential to do the same in the church.

- that the Spirit will open the eyes of disciples in your church to areas where they might need to lay down their rights or opinions in the name of love for their brothers and sisters.

- for the church to be a place that is known for people laying down their lives and willingly refusing to exercise their rights for the benefit of others, especially those who don't have the same privileges they have.

THE REMAINDER OF THE WEEK

Questions for Reflection

- Are there any areas revolving around the exercise of rights where Paul would challenge you to re-think your position or actions?

- Have you surrendered your rights to the way of the cross?

Application

- What is an application that you take away from this section for your faith community?

- What is the personal application that you take away from this section?

Further Study (Optional)

- Read the following article about idol meat in 1 Cor. 8: Sung Uk Lim, "The Political Economy of Eating Idol Meat: Practice, Structure, and Subversion in 1 Corinthians 8 through the Sociological Lens of Pierre Bourdieu," PDF (Academia.edu).

https://www.academia.edu/en/24574644/The_Political_Economy_of_Eating_Idol_Meat_Practice_Structure_and_Subversion_in_1_Corinthians_8_through_the_Sociological_Lens_of_Pierre_Bourdieu

1 CORINTHIANS 9:1–18

These animals accomplish their life and purpose in this world according to the incomprehensible will of the Creator. They render no account of their deeds because they are not rational. "Is God concerned about oxen?" Human beings, however, because they have been made rational, will render an account to God for themselves and for all the things which they have received for use in this present life.

—Fulgentius, 5th century AD

READ

—Read 1 Corinthians 9:1–18 out loud at least once.

—Read 1 Corinthians 9:1–18 at least once silently to yourself. Read it very slowly, allowing time for each word and phrase to resonate.

REFLECT

A Thought of Reflection

While Paul deals with various points of conflict and of the Corinthians acting according to their cultural training rather than kingdom standards, he continues to emphasize the folly of Christians choosing to prioritize their freedoms and rights. This is simply out of step for the new-creation community. To illustrate this clearly, Paul will show them that he practices what he preaches and does so in a costly way.

One of the rights that servants of the church had, like the apostles, was to be supported by the church when and where they needed it. Even though some still questioned Paul's apostleship, Corinth did not, and he had the right to garner financial support from them as he traveled to spread the gospel. Taking from both the secular and spiritual worlds, he gives several examples of those who labor reaping some of the harvests they produce. Paul's point is more than just that laborers deserve a wage; specifically, those who have given their lives to the gospel have the right to receive a living from the gospel. Yet he will go beyond his rights. It was not in their best interest for him to receive support from the Corinthian congregation because they were simply too spiritually immature to view it in the right way. They are still so conditioned by their culture that Paul fears they would twist the nature of their support and their subsequent relationship with him. So he will go beyond his rights and live out the self-sacrificing nature of the gospel, refusing for their benefit what would benefit him personally. There were some churches that Paul did accept support from, but that was not best for Corinth, so for their sake, he relishes the opportunity to make this choice in the name of the gospel.

But this was not about Paul boasting about himself. If Christians wanted to boast and establish their "status," they should do so by showing their weakness or by sacrificing in love for the good of others. His ongoing point is that this is what image-bearing communities look like. Personal rights in this kind of context were the wrong ground on which disciples should build a defense of their actions. Their foundation is Christ, and that meant laying down their privileges, upsetting the social structure, and creating a new reality for the world to see. And that is precisely what they had failed to do in this and many other areas of church life.

Preparation for Reflection

1. If Paul were writing to a contemporary church in America, do you think he would encourage personal rights knowing how important they are to our culture, or would his challenges to the church be even greater?

2. What are some specific behaviors revolving around personal freedoms and rights that Paul might rebuke a modern church for?

3. What do you think of Paul's statement that he would rather die than lose the boast of giving up his rights for the sake of the gospel and the good of his brothers and sisters? Does that anger or irritate you? Does it encourage you? Does it challenge you?

RECITE

Take 2–3 minutes to meditate on your own on the phrase, "But I have not used any of these rights." Listen for the Spirit to reveal new insights of understanding and application of this phrase to your life.

RESPOND

As you move into a time of prayer, focus on the things you normally pray for but today take some time to pray:

- that God's people will embrace the way of the cross and be willing to sacrifice their advantages, privileges, and rights for the sake of others.

- for the believers in your church to be willing to examine ways in which they might have been more influenced by the culture of personal rights than by the gospel.

- for those who have been wounded or hurt by other Christians who have emphasized their interests and failed to see ways in which they could live out the gospel.

THE REMAINDER OF THE WEEK

Questions for Reflection

- Who are some great examples in your church of people that sacrifice for the gospel and give up their rights for others? What can you learn from their example?

- Have there been times in the past when you could have sacrificed rights or comfort for the sake of your brothers and sisters but failed to do so? What can you learn from that?

Application

- What is an application that you take away from this section for your faith community?

- What is the personal application that you take away from this section?

Further Study (Optional)

- Read the following article about the gospel and Paul's rights: "The Woes of the Prophets and the Rights of the Apostle: The Internal Dynamics of 1 Corinthians 9" (JSTOR).

https://www.jstor.org/stable/43719406

1 CORINTHIANS 9:19-23

Did Paul merely pretend to be all things to all men, in the way
that flatterers do? No. He was a man of God and a doctor
of the spirit who could diagnose every pain, and with great
diligence, he tended them and sympathized with them all.
We all have something or other in common with everyone.
This empathy is what Paul embodied in dealing with each
particular person.

—Ambrosiaster, 4th century AD

READ

—Read 1 Corinthians 9:19–23 out loud at least once.
—Read 1 Corinthians 9:19–23 at least once silently to
yourself. Read it very slowly, allowing time for each word
and phrase to resonate.

REFLECT

A Thought of Reflection

In this passage, Paul lays out much more than merely
his approach to relationships. He has already urged the
believers in Corinth to imitate him in his approach to living
out the gospel (1 Corinthians 4:16), and that continues to be his
expectation. In living out the way of the cross, Paul knows that he is
indeed free. This was a meaningful term for those who were deeply
familiar with the benefits of status in Roman culture. Freedom was
highly prized, for the higher status you were, the more freedom you
had. Those of lower status had to be concerned with obedience and
humility, but not the free. So Paul highlights that he is indeed free
and belongs to no one to emphasize the fact that he willingly lays
that down and makes himself a slave to everyone. No one in Roman
culture would lower their status by choice, but that is precisely what
the way of the cross looks like. Why? To remove barriers and attract
as many to this new way of being a human and new way of living as
possible.

All the groups that Paul mentions that he is willing to identify with were outsiders in some respect. He made himself a slave, a group that was anathema to the free. To the Gentiles, the Jews were socially inferior. To those who were faithful observers of the law, people who did not live under the law were inferior. And to the strong, the weak were, well...weak. Paul is willing to be flexible and adaptable. He refuses to see categories of worth and advantage. To preserve societal privilege or status would be an affront to the gospel. He was "willing to associate with people of low position" (Rom. 12:16). That meant more than just being in their presence or attending the same church. Paul was willing to take on their lifestyle, see the world from their perspective, understand their culture, and live as equals with them.

Paul does this, he says, so that he may share in the blessings of the gospel. But what does he mean by that? Paul didn't believe that the gospel is just words. It is a lived reality. It is the restoration of image bearing where people of every nation and status level become one and live as equals as God intended all along for his creation. To be part of that is a vital aspect of the blessing of the gospel. But it demands giving of self. It means a willingness to die to ourselves, to give up our rights and preferences, and to embrace this new reality created by the gospel. It is not easy, but it is quite simple.

Preparation for Reflection

1. How does an overemphasis on personal rights serve as an obstacle to the gospel?

2. The Corinthian church was divided because they had left unexamined the social status divisions of their culture and accepted them into the life of the church. What versions of this same lie of superiority and privilege do we deal with in the contemporary context?

3. Why is it important to understand that the gospel is more than just words and a message to be believed but that it is also a life to be embodied?

RECITE

Take 2–3 minutes to meditate on your own on the phrase, "I have made myself a slave to everyone, to win as many as possible." Listen for the Spirit to reveal new insights of understanding and application of this phrase to your life.

RESPOND

As you move into a time of prayer, focus on the things you normally pray for but today take some time to pray:

- that God will help you desire to be a slave to all to embody the gospel and draw them to the radical way of life dictated by the gospel reality.

- that God will allow us to be a body that is truly willing to associate with people of low position in the fullest meaning of that concept.

- for those who may have been hurt and turned off from the gospel in the past because they did not find a community of people willing to be all things to all people.

THE REMAINDER OF THE WEEK

Questions for Reflection

- Am I willing to live as a slave to all?

- What does it mean for me to live for the sake of the gospel? How would I know if I am sharing in the blessings of the gospel?

Application

- What is an application that you take away from this section for your faith community?

- What is the personal application that you take away from this section?

Further Study (Optional)

- Read the following article about becoming all things to all people: Daniel P. Leyrer, "All Things to All People: An Exegetical Study of 1 Corinthians 9:19–23 with Application to North American Outreach" (coursehero.com).

https://www.coursehero.com/file/126612739/LeyrerAllpdf/

1 CORINTHIANS 9:24-27

Your master, Jesus Christ, has anointed you with his Spirit and has brought you to this training ground. He determined long before the day of the contest to take you from a softer way of life to a harsher regimen, that your strength may increase. Athletes are set apart for more rigid training to apply themselves to the building up of their physical strength. They are kept from lavish living, from more tempting dishes, from more pleasurable drinks. They are urged on, they are subjected to tortuous toils, they are worn out. The more strenuously they have exerted themselves, the greater is their hope of victory.

—Tertullian, 2nd century AD

READ

—Read 1 Corinthians 9:24–27 out loud at least once.
—Read 1 Corinthians 9:24–27 at least once silently to yourself. Read it very slowly, allowing time for each word and phrase to resonate.

REFLECT

A Thought of Reflection

Paul continues his explanation of why he has given up the right to take support from the Corinthians. It was not to offend or publicly insult them. Rather, Paul understood that the Corinthian disciples were still so influenced by the secular culture that his taking support would feed into their cultural expectation that he would then be indebted to them so they would have a great deal of influence in the specifics of his ministry. Therefore, this was part of the way of the cross and Paul's commitment to give up rights for the benefit of others. He gave up the right to receive support in the best interest of the church in Corinth, even if they couldn't yet understand that. And he gave up his rights and freedom for the benefit of living the gospel and drawing as many as possible to it.

Paul called the Corinthians to the life of the new creation, a life that gives up privileges, status, and comfort for the sake of the gospel and others. But he knows that this is not easy. He turns to the familiar world of sports to make his point. Athletes that succeed are the ones who put in the work and training to achieve their goals. Being all things to all people is not something that will simply happen because they have come to know Christ. They must follow the examples given to them; and at this point, they have failed spectacularly to do that. They have opted for the way of status and privilege, the way of self-concern, and the way laid out by the powers and authorities.

This is instructive for us today. We are prone to cultural values such as efficiency and ease. We want everything to be quick, painless, and as efficient as possible. But those simply aren't the qualities inherent to the way of the cross. It takes effort, thought, imagination, intentionality, hard work, perseverance, discipline, humility, and resolve. If Christianity is primarily about individuals developing a personal relationship with God, then little of this is truly necessary. But if God is forming a people that will live out the gospel, then self-sacrifice, self-emptying, and the surrender of rights are foundational to a life in Christ.

Preparation for Reflection

1. Why do you think Paul appealed to a metaphor from the sporting world to make his point here?

2. Why do you think that so many Christians are resistant to giving up our rights, intentionally seeing the world through the eyes of others and sacrificing our personal preferences and comfort zones for the sake of others?

3. What do you think Paul had in mind when he urged them to embrace strict training? What would that look like for someone desiring to embody the new creation?

RECITE

Take 2–3 minutes to meditate on your own on the phrase, "Run in such a way as to get the prize." Listen for the Spirit to reveal new insights of understanding and application of this phrase to your life.

RESPOND

As you move into a time of prayer, focus on the things you normally pray for but today take some time to pray:

• that God will make it clear to your church what rights might need to be sacrificed and what comfort zones must be abandoned to truly reflect the gospel.

• that God will grant humility to those who most need it in the body.

• for God's comfort to wash over those who have been marginalized in the body or not cared for in the way that they could have been.

THE REMAINDER OF THE WEEK

Questions for Reflection

• Am I willing to put in the work to be all things to all people?

• Do I understand the collective aspect of the Christian life, or do I overemphasize the individual part of being a Christian?

Application

• What is an application that you take away from this section for your faith community?

• What is the personal application that you take away from this section?

Further Study (Optional)

• Read the following article about the background of 1 Corinthians 9:24–27: "1 CORINTHIANS 9:24–27: AN AGONISTIC COMPETITION?" (JSTOR).

https://www.jstor.org/stable/43048415

1 CORINTHIANS 10:1–13

Once again, Paul casts down the pride of those who think they know it all. For if the Israelites, who had such great privileges, suffered these things, and if some were punished merely because they were heard to complain, how much more shall we suffer if we are not careful? Anyone who relies on himself will soon fall. The way in which we stand in this world is not secure and will not be until we are delivered out of the waves of this present life into the peaceful haven of eternal rest. Therefore, do not be proud of your standing, but pay attention so that you will not stumble. If Paul was afraid that it might happen to him, how much more ought we to be afraid also?

—Chrysostom, 4th century AD

READ

—Read 1 Corinthians 10:1–13 out loud at least once.
—Read 1 Corinthians 10:1–13 at least once silently to yourself. Read it very slowly, allowing time for each word and phrase to resonate.

REFLECT

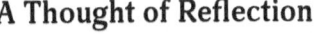

A Thought of Reflection

Throughout the letter to this point, Paul has dealt with contemporary issues within the culture and the problems that have been created by imitating the wisdom and systems of the world within the life of the church. Now he turns to an instance from Israel's past to teach an important lesson. The NIV translates the term Paul uses here as "examples," but the meaning of the word is more specific than that. Commentator Anthony Thiselton suggests that the term "formative models" is the best translation. What happened to Israel is a warning. The parallels are not exact, but there are enough similarities that the Christians can learn important lessons and change their behavior accordingly.

Israel underwent all the important markers to distinguish them as God's corporate people, including their own baptism of sorts and their own community-sustaining meal. Yet they let their desire for more carry them away. They did not control their cravings, and it led to rank disobedience and a failure to be God's agent in the world. This left them subject to the consequences of their behavior. The Christians in Corinth were also baptized and took communion, which identified and formed them as God's corporate people, but these were not magic talismans. They weren't saved by those things alone. They were saved by being God's agent in the world. They were the people that now stood in the overlap between the ages. The present was coming to an end but not yet. The age to come had broken in but not completely. This meant they must guard against the temptations of the present age while being comforted as citizens of the coming age, which helped protect against the doubt and anxiety brought on by the present age.

Through the use of the phrase or "crave" (NASB) and other indicators, Paul seems to be referring to chapter 8 and drawing comparisons to the lack of the strong submitting their rights but instead indulging in the high-status meals. They identified as followers of Jesus but failed to reckon with one of the most fundamental elements of being a disciple. If Israel fell through their desire for more, then so could they. But all was not hopeless. God had provided them with an escape from the temptation of this form of idolatry. Paul will get to that. But he still has a few more important examples to point out where they have failed to serve as true image-bearers before he gets to the solutions.

Preparation for Reflection

1. If Paul were to challenge today's church for collectively giving in to temptation and failing to represent God as his corporate ambassador, what do you think he might point out?

2. Why do you think Paul was so careful to call attention to the community identity points that marked Israel as God's people in terms that were easily identifiable with the

Christians' own identity markers before demonstrating how had they failed to be God's people?

3. In the context of this letter and Paul challenging the church about allowing cultural influence to direct church life, what do you think he meant by "No temptation has overtaken you [all] except something common to mankind" (NASB)?

RECITE

Take 2–3 minutes to meditate on your own on the phrase, "Do not be idolaters, as some of them were." Listen for the Spirit to reveal new insights of understanding and application of this phrase to your life.

RESPOND

As you move into a time of prayer, focus on the things you normally pray for but today take some time to pray:

•   that God will allow your church family to see areas where it needs to grow in being God's representative agent in the world.

•   for the church to be on guard against the temptation of mimicking and excusing the systemic and cultural sins of the world.

•   for God to reveal to your church family how you can be countercultural, where you can change, and how you can escape the wisdom of the world.

THE REMAINDER OF THE WEEK

Questions for Reflection

•   Do you live as God's representative agent, or have you let sinful cravings take over?

•   What can you do to help your church see the temptations from the culture that have had an impact on your church life?

Application

- What is an application that you take away from this section for your faith community?

- What is the personal application that you take away from this section?

Further Study (Optional)

- Read the following article about 1 Corinthians 10:1–13: Gary D. Collier, "'That We Might Not Crave Evil': The Structure and Argument of 1 Corinthians 10.1–13" (sagepub.com)

https://journals.sagepub.com/doi/abs/10.1177/0142064X9501705503

1 CORINTHIANS 10:14-22

Do you see how terribly Paul rebukes the Corinthians, shaking their very nerves and reducing them to an absurdity? Why, you may ask, did he not say this at the beginning? Because it is Paul's custom to prove his point by many details, placing the strongest last and prevailing in the argument by proving more than is strictly necessary. Thus, he began here with the smaller matters and made his way toward the greatest of evils so that the minds of the Corinthians had been prepared by the things already said. In this way, the last point is more easily absorbed.

—Chrysostom, 4th century AD

READ

—Read 1 Corinthians 10:14–22 out loud at least once.
—Read 1 Corinthians 10:14–22 at least once silently to yourself. Read it very slowly, allowing time for each word and phrase to resonate.

REFLECT

A Thought of Reflection

While Paul has been balanced throughout the discussion of loving one another and giving up rights to create a reality of image-bearing equality in the church in Corinth, he takes a more direct focus here aimed at the strong. Being people of the upper class meant that they had access to higher education and knowledge, which they had, at times, misapplied. So Paul challenges them as sensible (educated) people to judge for themselves. In other words, he charges them to decide between accessing either the wisdom of the world or spiritual wisdom. This is a return to the topic of chapter 8 and the exclusive meals that the strong were attending (and something Paul alluded to in the previous section).

The underlying notion that Paul presents here is that the wisdom of the world divides. It only sees the world through a limited perspective, so it cannot help but present only partial truth. The wisdom of God is different. It creates one out of many. That is what the Lord's Supper is all about. It is one loaf that serves to constantly transform a divided people into one body. It is part of the formation of the image-bearing community. The problem with the meals that feature meat sacrificed to idols is not the meat itself. The problem is not even that eating this meat is idolatry. What is idolatry and participation with demons is exalting one's rights to the point of dividing the body. The table of the Lord unites. The table of demons divides. And Paul wants them to use all the so-called knowledge they have gained due to their status to make a godly judgment.

It is challenging to determine how Paul's thoughts might be applied in a modern context. The real obstacle is that we can be just as prone to manipulating our status or privilege for our advantage yet remain completely blind to the ways in which we do it.

Preparation for Reflection

1. While he does remain as balanced and even-keeled as possible, why do you think Paul spends more time speaking directly to the strong than he does to the weak?

2. Why does Paul appeal to the Lord's Supper make his point about the role of rights in the life of privileged Christians?

3. If we often become blind to our culture's forms of preserving privilege and advantage, what steps can we take to become aware of those things?

RECITE

Take 2–3 minutes to meditate on your own on the phrase, "Flee from idolatry." Listen for the Spirit to reveal new insights of understanding and application of this phrase to your life.

RESPOND

As you move into a time of prayer, focus on the things you normally pray for but today take some time to pray:

- for the church to be increasingly free from the idolatry of using the world's wisdom and systems in the church.

- to be more aware of how we are influenced by and participate in the culture around us in ways that detract from truly being God's people.

- that God will continue to help the church grow in being a community of image-bearers so that we may be a light to the world in these difficult areas.

THE REMAINDER OF THE WEEK

 Questions for Reflection

- Do you ever choose your preference or convenience over what is good for brothers and sisters in your church? How would you go about gaining a perspective on that other than just your own?

- What does Paul mean when he says, "Are we trying to arouse the Lord's jealousy?"

Application

- What is an application that you take away from this section for your faith community?

- What is the personal application that you take away from this section?

Further Study (Optional)

- Read the following article about Paul's rhetorical use of the Lord's Supper: "The Social Background of 1 Corinthians 1–4," PDF (researchgate.net).

https://www.researchgate.net/publication/334591037_The_Social_Background_of_1_Corinthians_1-4

1 CORINTHIANS 10:23-11:1

It is true that anyone who is an idolater will seek what pleases him alone. He will place scandals in the way of the weaker brother's conscience. This is why we ought to be quick to resist doing just what we want to do, for the love of Christ and the salvation of our neighbors.

—Ambrosiaster, 4th century AD

READ

—Read 1 Corinthians 10:23–11:1 out loud at least once.
—Read 1 Corinthians 10:23–11:1 at least once silently to yourself. Read it very slowly, allowing time for each word and phrase to resonate.

REFLECT

A Thought of Reflection

Paul is now ready to summarize and move on from his exploration into the role of rights in the Christian community. Responsible, loving, and caring Christians will not take advantage of their liberty or rights if it damages the faith or inhibits the building up of other Christians. They will be people that understand that knowledge without love serves to puff up one's status, but it is love that builds others up (1 Corinthians 8:1). Liberty and rights are fine where they do not damage others or subject them to the effects of the great lie of status and superiority.

In this passage, Paul finishes with a specific example to tie up and put a bow on his larger point. If they are in a situation of being invited to a nonbeliever's house or a banquet and are served meat, they need not turn into a detective and determine the origins of the meat. They can simply show gratitude and enjoy it. The true issue is not the meat itself. What determines behavior is the other's conscience (a term that is probably better understood with biblical commentator Anthony Thiselton's suggestion of "self-awareness"). If another brother or sister (presumably) points out an issue with the meat, then it should be avoided. The guiding principle of my behavior is not my privileges, self-awareness, or access; in the community of image-bearers it becomes my concern for you. This is not the loss of freedom but the proper use of freedom. It is love for others that brings glory to God.

Paul calls the church in Corinth to the concept of viewing him as a pattern for this way of living, one that he patterned after Christ. Although most English translations render Paul's call here as one of following his example, "pattern" is a better translation because it conveys the idea that Paul wants them not just to copy what he is saying in specifically parallel situations. Rather, they are to apply the pattern of self-giving love and the way of the cross to every situation they encounter. Whether they are eating and drinking at a public meal or in whatever situation they find themselves, they are to live out the pattern of self-sacrifice and giving up rights for the benefit of others. In this way, self-giving becomes not just a singular action but the very identity of the church.

Preparation for Reflection

1. What balance does Paul strike between freedom and love for others in the body of Christ?

2. If eating meat that was sacrificed to idols was ultimately acceptable for a Christian, why do you think that Paul did not simply command everyone to eat meat and tell the weak-status Christians that they were wrong and needed to get educated on the subject?

3. In 1 Corinthians 8:13, Paul says that if what he eats were to cause another to fall into sin, he would never eat meat again. Why do you think he was so adamant about doing what builds up others over and above simply telling them what is right?

RECITE

Take 2–3 minutes to meditate on the phrase, "I am not seeking my own good but the good of many." Listen for the Spirit to reveal new insights of understanding and application of this phrase to your life.

RESPOND

As you move into a time of prayer, focus on the things you normally pray for but today take some time to pray:

- that God will help your church family to commit to actions that build up the body rather than indulge the self.

- that the Spirit will enlighten each member of the church to see areas where they should consider laying down their preferences for the sake of others.

- that God will help you desire to not seek your good but the good of others.

THE REMAINDER OF THE WEEK

 Questions for Reflection

- Do I have a pattern of thinking of the good of others before my good, rights, and preferences?

- What can I learn from Paul's principles in this passage that I can apply in my life?

Application

- What is an application that you take away from this section for your faith community?

- What is the personal application that you take away from this section?

Further Study (Optional)

- Read the following article about the imitation of Christ and what it meant for Paul: "Imitatio Christi (1 Corinthians 11:1): How Paul Imitates Jesus Christ in Dealing with Idol Food (1 Corinthians 8–10)" (re searchgate.net).

https://www.researchgate.net/publication/360237709_Imitatio_Christi_1_
Corinthians_111_How_Paul_Imitates_Jesus_Christ_in_Dealing_with_Idol_Food_1_
Corinthians_8-10

1 CORINTHIANS 11:2-16

If indeed, the goal of Christianity is the imitation of Christ according to the measure of his incarnation, insofar as is comfortable with the vocation of each individual, they who are entrusted with the guidance of many others are obliged to animate those still weaker than themselves, by their assistance to the imitation of Christ.

—Basil, 5th century AD

READ

—Read 1 Corinthians 11:2–16 out loud at least once.
—Read 1 Corinthians 11:2–16 at least once silently to yourself. Read it very slowly, allowing time for each word and phrase to resonate.

REFLECT

A Thought of Reflection

We are not sure of all the cultural specifics in this passage, and even the meaning is up for debate. Some assert that Paul was recommending that women cover their heads so as not to elicit cultural shame and create an obstacle to the gospel. In this view, some women were either emulating Roman elite "new women" by taking off head coverings (this was also something that prostitutes did, so it could have negative associations in either direction). Elite men covered their heads during religious ceremonies to signal their high status. Others insist that verses 7–10 are another example of Paul quoting the Corinthians before refuting this stance in verses 11–12 (otherwise the sentiments in these couplings seem contradictory). In this view, Paul is defending women against a group of men who were trying to keep women in their socially inferior spots by insisting that they cover their heads. Adding to this view is that both Paul and Peter encouraged women not to engage in the elaborate braided hairstyles of the economically elite (1 Timothy 2:9; 1 Peter 3:3), something that would be unnecessary if the normal

Christian practice (v. 16) were for women to wear head coverings.

Another confusing aspect of this passage is the reference to the head and what that metaphor means. The most culturally consistent understanding would be that "head" refers to the public face or representative of the family.

What is clearer in this passage is that it is about respect. Paul calls the believers to show respect for one another and God by not taking actions that would bring unnecessary shame to the community or serve as an obstacle to the spread of the gospel. They should not try to flaunt their status or demean the status of others. Paul encouraged the freedom of women to pray and prophesy in public worship but not to become so enamored with demonstrating this status publicly that it would signal disrespect to others. There is much that we don't know for certain about this situation, but what is certain is that whatever the specifics of the situation in Corinth at the time, Paul was calling for an embodiment of an image-bearing community that emphasized love and honor for all.

Preparation for Reflection

1. Why is it important to see that in some instances, like this passage, we simply do not know exactly what the situation was that Paul was addressing and can only responsibly see general principles rather than specific practices?

2. What does Paul mean when he asserts that woman is not independent of man, nor is man independent of woman?

3. What can we learn from the fact that Paul would analyze even what people wore in worship to ensure that they were not exercising their freedoms and benefits over the good of the body and demonstrating the gospel to others?

RECITE

Take 2–3 minutes to meditate on your own on the phrase, "In the Lord woman is not independent of man, nor is man independent of woman." Listen for the Spirit to reveal new insights of understanding and application of this phrase to your life.

RESPOND

As you move into a time of prayer, focus on the things you normally pray for but today take some time to pray:

- for the church to grow in humility.

- for the leaders to grow in humility.

- for you to grow in humility.

THE REMAINDER OF THE WEEK

Questions for Reflection

- Are there any ways in which we can subtly demonstrate our status or level of attainment in gatherings of the body?

- What can I do to bring greater unity to my small group this week?

Application

- What is an application that you take away from this section for your faith community?

- What is the personal application that you take away from this section?

Further Study (Optional)

- Read the following article about head coverings in Corinth: "Honour, Head-Coverings and Headship: 1 Corinthians 11.2–16 in Its Social Context" (DocsLib).

https://docslib.org/doc/1027549/honour-head-coverings-and-headship-1-corinthians-11-2-16-in-its-social-context

1 CORINTHIANS 11:17-26

The Lord's Supper is the sacrament of the Lord. Everyone participates equally in it, whether they are poor or rich, slaves or lords, rulers or ruled. Common tables must at all costs be truly common so as to imitate the table of the Lord, which is open to all equally.

—Theodoret of Cyrrhus, 5th century AD

READ

—Read 1 Corinthians 11:17–26 out loud at least once.
—Read 1 Corinthians 11:17–26 at least once silently to yourself. Read it very slowly, allowing time for each word and phrase to resonate.

REFLECT

A Thought of Reflection

Imagine having an apostle of the gospel tell you that your gatherings for the Lord's Supper were doing more harm than good. What did Paul mean by that? The Corinthian believers gathered regularly for a common meal and celebration of what we call the Lord's Supper or communion. But in doing so, they were leaving many of their normal cultural practices unexamined. Wealthier disciples who did not work and had plenty of leisure time were seemingly starting the meal early, likely eating together in the banquet room known as the triclinium and eating high-quality food. The hardworking lower class and slaves would not be able to come until later in the evening, would likely eat in the outer courts, would have little to no food, and their food would be of lower quality. If the food was provided, those of high status would naturally have better quality and a higher quantity of food served to them. None of this would have seemed out of place.

What they were failing to do was to be people of the new

creation. They were acting like the world around them. They were assuming that it was every person for themselves. They did not question the idea that people had rights to their own economic and social status and nothing less or nothing more. They might have felt quite proud of their actions. After all, they were a diverse church. They were a collection of strong and weak that were meeting together. But diversity by itself is not what the gospel is about. Image bearing includes equality, or as Paul would detail in his next letter to the Corinthians, "The goal is equality, as it is written, 'The one who gathered too much did not have too much, and the one who gathered little did not have too little'" (2 Corinthians 8:14b–15).

There will always be differences in the diverse body of Christ, but there do not have to be hierarchies, status levels, and divisions that mimic the lie of superiority and inferiority from the surrounding culture. There cannot be a state of leaving unexamined the purpose of the body. Proclaiming the Lord's death means being a visible icon of the new-creation community established by his death to collectively live according to the self-emptying way of the cross. If the message is sent during our gatherings that things like status, power, wealth, and class still have an effect on our common life, then our meetings may be doing more harm to the gospel than good.

Preparation for Reflection

1. The Corinthians were reflecting the sin of status division in their meetings. Can you think of any contemporary division that can have a visible or tangible impact on our gatherings in a similar way?

2. Why do you think Paul uses such extreme language, saying that they are doing more harm than good and are even humiliating the weak?

3. Why does Paul think that things like where, what, and when they were eating made a difference or mattered at all when it came to partaking in the Lord's Supper?

RECITE

Take 2–3 minutes to meditate on your own on the phrase, "You proclaim the Lord's death until he comes." Listen for the Spirit to reveal new insights of understanding and application of this phrase to your life.

RESPOND

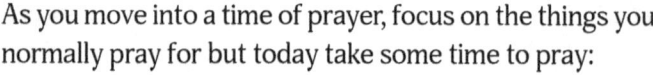

As you move into a time of prayer, focus on the things you normally pray for but today take some time to pray:

- that God will help your church become aware of any contemporary examples of not living out the equality of the image-bearing community.

- that God will grant us great patience, grace, and love toward one another.

- that God will also grant us great persistence and perseverance to see and deal with any inequities in the body that reflect the cultural sin around us.

THE REMAINDER OF THE WEEK

Questions for Reflection

- How does the collective life of my small group and church declare the Lord's death?

- Are there any ways in which I have accepted or become blind to divisions in the body?

Application

- What is an application that you take away from this section for your faith community?

- What is the personal application that you take away from this section?

Further Study (Optional)

- Read the following article about social conflict and communion in Corinth: "Social Identity and Conflict in Corinth: 1 Corinthians 11.17–34 in Context" (whiterose.ac.uk)

https://eprints.whiterose.ac.uk/96447/7/Final%20copy%2C%20Finney%20Social%20 Identity%20and%20Conflict%20in%20Corinth.pdf

[Note: The following quote is a commentary on 1 Corinthians 11 and on the urgent need for each church to address situations like the one Paul teaches here.] Judge in yourself what I am going to tell you: Suppose you happen to go on a long journey and, parched with thirst in the heat, you chance upon one of the brothers. You say to him, "Refresh me in my exhaustion from thirst," and he replies, "It is the time for prayer; I will pray and then I will come to your aid"; and while he is praying, before coming to you, you die of thirst. What seems to you the better, that he should go and pray, or alleviate your exhaustion?

—Aphrahat, 4th century AD

READ

—Read 1 Corinthians 11:23–34 out loud at least once.
—Read 1 Corinthians 11:23–34 at least once silently to yourself. Read it very slowly, allowing time for each word and phrase to resonate.

REFLECT

A Thought of Reflection

This section continues Paul's scathing rebuke of the Corinthian congregation for their enactment of the Lord's Supper. Rather than being a body of new creation and proclaiming the power of the Lord's death by being one body, they were instead reflecting the divisions of the world. They were blind to all this, but that was a major element of Paul's point. They did not see that the divisions of their culture had embedded themselves into the life of the church because the strong did not want to see. Even though they would likely have claimed to be status-blind, they were quite the opposite.

Paul says they were taking the bread and cup in an unworthy manner. How so? By maintaining the social structures, inequities, and divisions of the great lie of human superiority and inferiority. They were not perpetrating those attitudes and structures themselves. But they were allowing them to infect and remain in the church. They lacked the courage necessary to carefully examine themselves. They were partaking of the Lord's body (in communion) without discerning the Lord's body (the church), Paul says, in a clever play on words. They had a choice, though. They could either engage in the painful work of seeing their own biases and becoming aware of how they were allowing their brothers and sisters to be subjected to the structures and inequities of their age (effectively blocking them from experiencing the life of the new creation), or they could stand before God, answer to him, and be condemned with the world.

The passage itself makes clear that Paul is not talking simply about the personal examination of individual sin but the larger issues of status division when he encourages them to all eat together. If they are going to claim to be the body of Christ, then they must act that way. Paul's challenge here is especially relevant to the contemporary church. Do we subject brothers and sisters to the sin of the world through economic, status, class, social, national, racial, or other inequities that we refuse to examine among ourselves?

Preparation for Reflection

1. Why does Paul think that it is so important for every Christian to examine their attitudes and actions toward the body as they take communion?

2. If Paul were challenging the contemporary church for allowing the divisions of the world to impact the church, what specific areas might he point out?

3. Why do you think it was so difficult for the Corinthians to see the sin of division and status that had taken hold in their church?

RECITE

Take 2–3 minutes to meditate on your own on the phrase, "Everyone ought to examine themselves." Listen for the Spirit to reveal new insights of understanding and application of this phrase to your life.

RESPOND

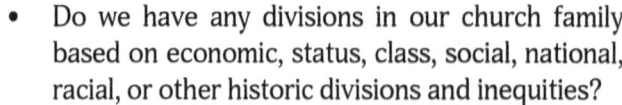

As you move into a time of prayer, focus on the things you normally pray for but today take some time to pray:

- that we will be willing to undertake the uncomfortable and even painful work of self-examination rather than face God's judgment for failure to do so.

- that the Spirit will guide us into the courage needed to be honest about areas where we have allowed the divisions of the world along the lines of privilege and status to affect us.

- that we will be willing to embrace our present situation by trusting the perspective of others and seeing things through their eyes as much as possible.

THE REMAINDER OF THE WEEK

Questions for Reflection

- Do we have any divisions in our church family based on economic, status, class, social, national, racial, or other historic divisions and inequities?

- What can I do to see the situation through the eyes of those who have had very different experiences than I have?

Application

- What is an application that you take away from this section for your faith community?

- What is the personal application that you take away from this section?

Further Study (Optional)

- Read the following article about the importance of a socially equitable communion table: "The Lord's Supper? When eating and dining become determinative in 1 Corinthians 11:17–34" (ScienceGate).

https://www.sciencegate.app/document/10.1177/0034637320969415

1 CORINTHIANS 12:1–11

DAY 26

We are all the body of Christ, whose head is God, whose members we are. Some perhaps are like the eyes, like the prophets. Others are more like teeth, as the apostles who passed the food of the gospel teaching into our hearts.... Some are hands who are seen carrying out good works. Those who bestow the strength of nourishment upon the poor are his belly. Some are his feet, and would that I was worthy to be his heel! He pours water on the feet of Christ who forgives the lowly their sins, and, in setting free the common man, he bathes the feet of Christ.

—Ambrose, 4th century AD

READ

—Read 1 Corinthians 12:1–11 out loud at least once.
—Read 1 Corinthians 12:1–11 at least once silently to yourself. Read it very slowly, allowing time for each word and phrase to resonate.

REFLECT

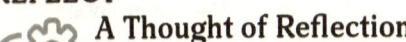

A Thought of Reflection

The continuing theme of 1 Corinthians helps us to locate and understand Paul's direction in this passage. Theologian and historian Bruce Winter put forth an extremely compelling case that verse 3 should be understood as the Corinthians using the name of Jesus to curse rivals rather than to curse Jesus. This was the standard pagan practice of the day—to use the name and authority of one's god to gain status and social advantage (really, any kind of advantage) over others. This is part of the pattern of copying the ways of the culture that resulted in rivalries and divisions within the body of Christ and runs in the opposite direction of a community where everyone affirms that Jesus is King.

This desire to use every situation to their own advantage (cf. Phil. 2:6) was even evident in their approach to spiritual gifts. The distribution of gifts was done by God for the good of the whole church. What gift someone had been given was of little matter. What mattered was that they would act as stewards of that gift and utilize it for the benefit of others, not to establish and increase their status and standing. It was not their role to select which gifts they would have, and it was certainly not in their purview to rank the gifts in importance. The moment they did that was the moment that they began to rank one another in order of value to the community. And doing that would be the exact opposite of what an image-bearing community should look like.

Paul's reminder for the Corinthians here should guide us toward introspection. We may not find value and worth from all the same spiritual gifts listed, but we should examine ourselves to see if there are some spiritual gifts, roles, or positions that do tempt us toward finding value in the gifts God has given us and then subtly ranking them. Do we find those gifted with speaking to be more important in the body than those with the gift of caring for the outcast and marginalized? Do those with gifts of leadership get ranked higher in the minds of many than those gifted in behind-the-scenes work?

Preparation for Reflection

1. Why did Paul began this section with why we need one another in the body with a reminder that we cannot use Jesus as a curse formula to gain an advantage over rivals?

2. Why does Paul emphasize that though there are different types of gifts, it is the same Lord, the same Spirit, and the same God?

3. What might some parallel situations to this look like in the modern church where people, both leaders and non-leaders, find importance and value over other Christians based on what they do in the body or how they are gifted?

RECITE

Take 2–3 minutes to meditate on your own on the phrase, "The manifestation of the Spirit is given for the common good." Listen for the Spirit to reveal new insights of understanding and application of this phrase to your life.

RESPOND

As you move into a time of prayer, focus on the things you normally pray for but today take some time to pray:

- that those who have not been using their gifts for the benefit of the body would seek ways to do so.

- that the church will grow in utilizing and celebrating the gifts of all members.

- that the body will be willing to humbly examine whether it sometimes has given in to the temptation to subtly rank gifts and positions according to worth and value.

THE REMAINDER OF THE WEEK

Questions for Reflection

- Do I use my gifts to their fullest extent to build up the body?

- Do I act as if I believe some gifts or roles are more important than others?

Application

- What is an application that you take away from this section for your faith community?

- What is the personal application that you take away from this section?

Further Study (Optional)

- Read the following article on social status and spiritual gifts: "The 'Ultracharismatics' of Corinth and the Pentecostals of Latin America as the Religion of the Disaffected," PDF (researchgate.net)

https://www.researchgate.net/publication/325273941_The_%27Ultracharismatics%27_of_Corinth_and_the_Pentecostals_of_Latin_America_as_the_Religion_of_the_Disaffected

1 CORINTHIANS 12:12-20

DAY 27

*Even if the body had only its most important member, it
would still be useless without the others.*
—Theodoret of Cyrrhus, 5th century AD

READ

—Read 1 Corinthians 12:12–20 out loud at least once.
—Read 1 Corinthians 12:12–20 at least once silently to
yourself. Read it very slowly, allowing time for each word
and phrase to resonate.

REFLECT

A Thought of Reflection

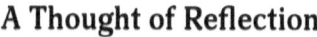

From his first encounter with the risen Christ on the way
to Damascus, Paul learned that Christ and his people are
inseparable. On the way to hunt down Christians, Paul
was confronted by Jesus, who asked him, "Why do you persecute
me?" He took that lesson to heart, asserting here that Christians are
the very limbs and organs of Christ. This means that to mistreat,
overlook, or sin against a brother or sister was more than just a
matter of social preference. This was of the utmost importance to
the reality and function of the family of Christ.

For half a millennium, Roman writers had utilized the imagery
of the body to emphasize the need for respect of the hierarchy,
stressing that the non-elites and those of lower status were there to
serve the elites, who depended on their labor. This was how society
must function for the good of all. Paul completely flipped that on
its head. Those of low status should never think of themselves as
unnecessary, unneeded, or a burden to the body. And those of
high status should not either. The non-elites need the support of
their higher-status siblings in Christ. The more privileged should
be looking for ways to see life from their perspective, share in their
struggles, and lift them from their circumstances. What would it
take for the mindsets, structures, and systems of the surrounding

culture to be upturned so that in the community of the new creation, the marginalized would be honored and respected as equal parts of the body? If done properly, this would not be in a paternalistic or condescending way. It would entail genuine efforts to right the wrongs of their society and to erase the advantages created by the lie of the superiority of status.

It can be very easy to subtly begin to believe that it would be preferable to be in a church of those who have experienced what we have in life, who hold similar perspectives and values, and who are like us in important identity markers. That is why Paul stresses that God has designed it the way he did. Yes, it would be easier to group up with those like us, but that would not be a display of God's wisdom. It would not be a defeat of the powers and authorities. There is one Spirit who brought us into common allegiance as members that belong to one another. Just embracing this as our true identity is challenging enough. But Paul is heading somewhere vitally important with this argument, and the deepest challenges are yet to come.

Preparation for Reflection

1. Why does Paul stress the oneness of the Spirit and the oneness of the body of Christ?

2. What might induce those who are seen as low-status, un-important, or marginalized in society to feel that they do not belong to the body? What are some of the factors that could contribute to that?

3. What are some of the important implications of Paul's assertion that every part of the body has been placed exactly as God wanted it?

RECITE

Take 2–3 minutes to meditate on your own on the phrase, "There are many parts, but one body." Listen for the Spirit to reveal new insights of understanding and application of this phrase to your life.

RESPOND

As you move into a time of prayer, focus on the things you normally pray for but today take some time to pray:

- that everyone in the body would feel welcomed, loved, and valued.

- that those with societal advantages would not feel ashamed, guilty, or defensive about them or be tempted to deny it but would instead view it as a gift from God to be shared with others to display God's wisdom and glory.

- for those who have left the body of Christ in the past because they felt overlooked or unloved.

THE REMAINDER OF THE WEEK

Questions for Reflection

- Am I willing to share any cultural or societal privilege I might have with those who do not?

- Have I ever unintentionally made someone in the body feel unwelcome or unvalued?

Application

- What is an application that you take away from this section for your faith community?

- What is the personal application that you take away from this section?

Further Study (Optional)

- Read the following article on body and belly metaphors in Roman literature and Paul's writing: "Why Paul's Fabulous Body Is Missing Its Belly: The Rhetorical Subversion of Menenius Agrippa's Fable in 1 Corinthians 12.12–30" (researchgate.net)

https://www.researchgate.net/publication/328004369_Why_Paul's_Fabulous_Body_is_Missing_its_Belly_The_Rhetorical_Subversion_of_Menenius_Agrippa's_Fable_in_1_Corinthians_1212-30

1 CORINTHIANS 12:21-30

Paul points out that if division in the body is to be avoided, greater attention must be given to the lesser parts so that they will not be harmed or feel excluded. If they were badly treated, they would be destroyed, and their destruction would be the ruin of the body.

—Chrysostom, 4th century AD

READ

—Read 1 Corinthians 12:21–30 out loud at least once.
—Read 1 Corinthians 12:21–30 at least once silently to yourself. Read it very slowly, allowing time for each word and phrase to resonate.

REFLECT

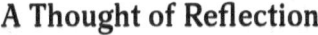

A Thought of Reflection

Having gone through myriad examples of the Corinthian congregation failing to be the embodiment of the new creation and the body of Christ that they have been called to be, Paul begins pointing them to the solutions to their problems. There might be a temptation to think that they didn't need one another. The weak might think that they are mistreated by the strong or grow envious of them and believe they would be better off without the indignities and without being overlooked or misunderstood. The strong might see the weak as a burden or as trying to take advantage of them. Paul emphasizes in verse 21 that the higher parts of the body cannot say that they don't need the lower parts like the hands or feet. They are indispensable.

Beginning in verse 23, Paul turns the world upside down. Those who are marginalized or treated inequitably in the world will be treated with special honor in the body. Those with honor and privilege in the world need no special treatment. This is not favoritism, says Paul. It has been planned this way by God to bring the equity and dignity of the new creation into the present age. It won't come through determination, hard work, sweat, or the discipline of the weak. It will come by the body lifting those who had been treated as inferior by the world. Treating the weak with special thought and intentional honor, says Paul, is the way that there will be no divisions. Society and the great lie of superiority have already created divisions. Without intentional action, the church will simply mimic those divisions, even if they take a slightly nicer form, are more subtle, or are less spoken of. They are there. Each part of the body should learn to see the world through the eyes of the other, care for the other, and work toward the equity of image bearing (see 2 Corinthians 8–9 where Paul demonstrates what this looks like on an economic scale). If one part of the body is subjected to suffering and lack of honor, then that is the concern of the whole body. Everyone of every status should take that position on themselves. They should not be ashamed to associate themselves with people of low position as if that were their own status (Romans 12:16). If one part of the body, in this case, the weak, is lifted and shown honor, then that is an honor for the whole community.

Our task here once again is to understand the original context and situation and then carefully apply Paul's guidance to our situations and versions of the great lie. It will not be easy, but it is central to being people of the gospel and understanding the role that we are to have in the body of Christ and the world

Preparation for Reflection

1. To truly be able to associate with people of lower social status and suffer with those who suffer, what responsibility does that put on the strong?

2. Why does Paul call for the weak to be treated with special honor while arguing that the strong need no special treatment? Why is this not favoritism?

3. What are some parallel situations in today's church that Paul's guidance might be applied to, and what would it look like to heed his wisdom?

RECITE

Take 2–3 minutes to meditate on your own on the phrase, "God has put the body together, giving greater honor to the parts that lacked it." Listen for the Spirit to reveal new insights of understanding and application of this phrase to your life.

RESPOND

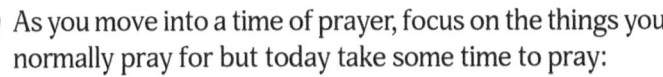

As you move into a time of prayer, focus on the things you normally pray for but today take some time to pray:

- that God will help you be guided by the wisdom of his world rather than the wisdom of the culture or the norms that you are used to or have believed are the right things to do.

- that God will help your church give greater honor to the parts that have lacked it in the world.

- that the Spirit will guide your church into a fellowship that truly identifies with one another and is willing to experience the world in solidarity with one another.

THE REMAINDER OF THE WEEK

Questions for Reflection

- What can I do to be part of a church that turns social divisions into the equity of the new creation by giving special honor to the socially weak?

- Are there any ways in which I have contributed to the divisions of the world becoming divisions in the body of Christ, even if it has been by ignoring the plight of those historically treated as inferior by the surrounding culture?

Application

- What is an application that you take away from this section for your faith community?

- What is the personal application that you take away from this section?

Further Study (Optional)

 • Read the following article about the social pecking order of the ancient world: "Ancient History: Social Pecking Order in the Roman World" (BBC History).

https://www.bbc.co.uk/history/ancient/romans/social_structure_01.shtml

In other words, says Paul, if I have no love, I am not just use-less but a positive nuisance.

—Chrysostom, 4th century AD

READ

—Read 1 Corinthians 12:31–13:13 out loud at least once.
—Read 1 Corinthians 12:31–13:13 at least once silently to yourself. Read it very slowly, allowing time for each word and phrase to resonate.

REFLECT

A Thought of Reflection

This is one of the most beloved and well-known passages of Scripture. Yet it is also one of the passages most separated from its context within the letter of 1 Corinthians. This is a beautiful passage that can and should rightly be applied to myriad secondary contexts and situations. But to be able to properly utilize secondary applications of a text, we must first understand its place and function in the original context. That is particularly true with this passage. Paul has been painstakingly showing the Corinthian congregation how they have allowed the great lie of superiority to take root in their lives together before launching into the principles of resolving that situation in the previous chapter. One effect of believing the great lie was that they were using spiritual gifts to compete and establish status. Paul wishes them to see that the greater gifts are faith, hope, and love. But love is the greatest. It is the very foundation of who they are as the people of God.

Without love, they could have the most impressive of the spiritual gifts at the highest levels but would be a detriment to the church rather than an addition. Take note that Paul does not offer an exhaustive list of the characteristics of love. He emphasizes the qualities that are especially relevant to the divisions of status. Among the other important qualities that he highlights, Paul says that love for others means that they will not envy the position of one another; they will not boast and work to establish status or advantage over others; they will not take steps to dishonor or treat others as inferior; they will not seek their good but put the interests of others ahead of their own; they will trust or believe the best about others, and they will never give up. Other gifts are limited and will not always be needed in the body, but love will never pass away. Even when the perfect age to come finally arrives, love will be the central component.

In the early part of this letter, Paul chided them for acting like children because they were competing for status, which is the opposite of love. Now he urges them to put away childish things, just as he did, and act maturely. He wants them to live on earth as though they were already in God's presence (Mt. 6:10). God has ordered the body by putting the strong and weak together, and the strong are to willingly share their privilege and status with the weak. That is tangible love. We should not miss Paul's obvious implication in all of this. If they fail to give greater honor to the parts that lack it and suffer with those who suffer, then they do not love their brothers and sisters.

Preparation for Reflection

1. Why do you think Paul emphasizes love as the key to combating divisions in the body of Christ?

2. Why do you think Paul chose to start his description of love with the idea of being "patient"?

3. What is Paul's point in connecting knowing fully and being fully known with the community expression of love?

RECITE

Take 2–3 minutes to meditate on your own on the phrase, "Love never fails." Listen for the Spirit to reveal new insights of understanding and application of this phrase to your life.

RESPOND

As you move into a time of prayer, focus on the things you normally pray for but today take some time to pray:

- that God will help you to put more effort into loving others.

- for your church to be committed to living out the practical actions of love that Paul has been describing throughout this letter.

- to grow more in your understanding of love as the central aspect of church life.

THE REMAINDER OF THE WEEK

Questions for Reflection

- What can you do specifically to demonstrate love in the body of Christ this week?

- Do I, at times, act in the body of Christ with a motivation other than love?

Application

- What is an application that you take away from this section for your faith community?

- What is the personal application that you take away from this section?

Further Study (Optional)

- Read the following article about the context of 1 Corinthians 13: Steven L. Cox, "1 Corinthians 13—An Antidote to Violence: Love" (sagepub.com).

https://journals.sagepub.com/doi/abs/10.1177/003463739609300408

1 CORINTHIANS 14:1–12

A person is built up when he finds out the answer to disputed points. Encouragement comes to him when he is enabled to endure. He is consoled when he continues in hope even when others are viewing his discipline with contempt. Knowledge of the law strengthens his soul and encourages him to hope for better things.

—Ambrosiaster, 4th century AD

READ

—Read 1 Corinthians 14:1–12 out loud at least once.
—Read 1 Corinthians 14:1–12 at least once silently to yourself. Read it very slowly, allowing time for each word and phrase to resonate.

REFLECT

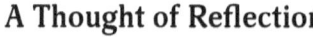

A Thought of Reflection

Paul has shown how the Corinthians must be willing to show love by putting the interests of others ahead of their own. This includes building up the body rather than working to bring advantage to oneself. Throughout this chapter, Paul demonstrates the love he described in chapter 13 and shows how it will cause them to approach things like the use of spiritual gifts and the ordering of church life and worship as a means to build up the church rather than to bring status to individuals. It is not bad to desire spiritual gifts, unless the motivation is competition and boasting. If they follow the way of love in any aspect of church life, they will be on the right track.

Using the example of the gift of speaking in languages or prophesying is a perfect vehicle to demonstrate what love looks like in their real lives. The Roman culture would have them squeeze the gifts for self-advantage and advancement. They should utilize gifts to impress others. That would lead them to highly prize the gift of languages, just as they had done, because it was showy and impressive. Prophesying was less so. It seems that more people could do it, and it didn't appear so miraculous. Whether Paul refers here to the ability to praise God in a language that the speaker had not learned or to speak in an unknown language (although the writings of the early church indicate that they understood Paul to be referring to known languages that the speaker could not understand and had never learned), Paul's point is that speaking in languages, if not interpreted, did nothing for people who could not understand them. It made the speaker look super spiritual but did nothing to build up the church (1 Corinthians 10:23–24). Prophecy, however, very much encouraged, informed, and strengthened the body.

Although Paul is using these gifts as an example, his overall point is much larger and is a practical illustration of what he has been teaching throughout the letter. They should not mimic the values of the world and pursue position, privilege, and status. Whether they eat, drink, or utilize spiritual gifts, it should be for the glory of God and the benefit of the church. Most humans don't like to give up privileges. We defend them. We deny that we have them so that we don't risk losing them. We resist equality because when all you've ever known is an advantage, equality feels like oppression. But Paul consistently and unwaveringly calls them, and each one of us, to the way of the cross.

Preparation for Reflection

1. In the modern era of the church, there is much attention on finding fulfillment through finding your spiritual gifting. How does Paul's wisdom here serve as an important barrier to abusing that concept?

2. Why does Paul specifically value the gift of prophecy over the gift of speaking in languages?

3. What are some specific contemporary examples of people engaging in spiritual things that are good in and of themselves but misusing them for their benefit rather than for the good of others?

RECITE

Take 2–3 minutes to meditate on your own on the phrase, "Try to excel in those that build up the church." Listen for the Spirit to reveal new insights of understanding and application of this phrase to your life.

RESPOND

As you move into a time of prayer, focus on the things you normally pray for but today take some time to pray:

- that every member of the church will use the gifts the Spirit has apportioned to them to benefit of the body.

- that the body will excel at encouraging one another.

- that your church will be increasingly known for its genuine love for one another.

THE REMAINDER OF THE WEEK

Questions for Reflection

- Do I use the gifts and strengths that I possess to build others up rather than to benefit myself?

- How can I use my spiritual gifts and strengths even more for the benefit of the body of Christ?

Application

- What is an application that you take away from this section for your faith community?

- What is the personal application that you take away from this section?

Further Study (Optional)

- Read this article on the connection between prophecy and modern preaching: Chris Knights, "Prophecy and Preaching: Does What Paul Calls 'Prophecy' in 1 Corinthians 14 Include What We Would Today Call 'Preaching'?" (sagepub.com).

https://journals.sagepub.com/doi/10.1177/0014524618784490

1 CORINTHIANS 14:13-25

DAY 31

Paul wants them to be mature intellectually so they will grasp accurately what is needed for the upbuilding of the church. In this way they will leave behind malice and errors, striving instead for the things which are conducive to the good of the brotherhood.

—Ambrosiaster, 4th century AD

READ

—Read 1 Corinthians 14:13–25 out loud at least once.

—Read 1 Corinthians 14:13–25 at least once silently to yourself. Read it very slowly, allowing time for each word and phrase to resonate.

REFLECT

A Thought of Reflection

To understand what Paul is saying to the Corinthians in this passage, it is important to grasp that his main concern is with uttering words that no one, including the speaker, understands. It makes no difference whether Paul is referring to speaking known languages or ecstatic utterances. The main point is that they were doing it without interpretation to display a showy and impressive spiritual gift that benefited no one. This is childish behavior aimed at exalting one's status and looking important in the eyes of others. These are the values of the surrounding culture, not what image-bearers should desire. Instead, he wants them to be mature in their thinking and strive for gifts and practices that will build up the church and benefit others.

What Paul says in verses 20–25 can be quite confusing but is rather important to deciphering his point for the church. He points to Isaiah 28 at a time when Israel was in exile, and hearing people's languages that they did not know was a sign of their judgment. That is not the situation that God's people should be in, but when anyone engages in gifts that don't benefit others, like speaking words that no one understands, they put them in that position. If someone were to come in and hear everyone uttering words that no one could understand, it would be processed by those in the culture as something like the ecstatic utterances of many of the pagan religions. Stephen Chester has convincingly argued that saying, "You are out of your mind" was not a putdown in the way we would mean it. It was a recognition that one had the gift of spiritual madness and the ability to utter profound spiritual mysteries. In other words, it would have looked just like the surrounding pagan religions. Thus, speaking unintelligible words meant putting others in the position of exile or unbeliever and signaled to the culture that the believers were no different from the people around them.

But prophecies were to encourage, challenge, and build up the church. If that same visitor came in and heard that, it would be a sign that they were among a different sort of people. They would see a sign that was for believers. It would show the visitor that they were in the presence of the people of the new creation—image-bearers who were in the very presence of God. The Christians in Corinth had failed to see that their self-glorifying behavior was immature, displayed the signs of being a people under judgment rather than believers, and could serve as an obstacle for others to come into the kingdom of God.

Preparation for Reflection

1. Why is Paul so against behavior that lifts the self-esteem of individuals but does nothing to benefit the body?

2. Can you think of a contemporary scenario where a Christian might use a spiritual gift to puff up their reputation or level of prestige, but rather than impressing others, it leaves outsiders feeling like Christians are no different from anyone else and leave believers feeling inferior to the one displaying such puffed-up behavior?

3. What does Paul mean when he says that he would rather speak five intelligible words to instruct than ten thousand in a different language?

RECITE

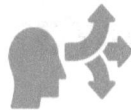

Take 2–3 minutes to meditate on the phrase, "God is really among you!" Listen for the Spirit to reveal new insights of understanding and application of this phrase.

RESPOND

As you move into a time of prayer, focus on the things you normally pray for but today take some time to pray:

- that God will guide your church into greater maturity and love for one another.

- that God will give more and more gifts to the church that will help to build it up in love.

- that those who visit your congregation will truly see that God is among you.

THE REMAINDER OF THE WEEK

Questions for Reflection

- If someone were to come and experience the ethos and life of my small group, would it seem just like any other group in the world, or would they say, "God is among you"?

- What is the connection that Paul draws between self-giving love and the presence of God? What does that mean for our church and for me?

Application

- How can this be applied to your faith community?

- What is the personal application that you take away from this section?

Further Study (Optional)

- Read this article about languages and prophecy: "'By the Lips of Foreigners': Disclosing the Church in 1 Corinthians 14:20–25" (researchgate.net)

https://www.researchgate.net/publication/328326386_'By_the_Lips_of_Foreigners'_Disclosing_the_Church_in_1_Corinthians_1420-25

Truly, the church was more like heaven in Paul's time, because the Spirit governed everything and moved each one of the members in turn. But now it seems we have only the symbols of those gifts. We also have only two or three speaking in the service, but these are only a pale shadow of what prevailed then. The present church is like a woman who has fallen from her former, prosperous days and who retains only the outward signs of that prosperity, displaying the boxes and caskets in which she kept her wealth, but which are now empty. This is true not only in the matter of gifts but in life and virtue as well.

—Chrysostom, 4th century AD

READ

—Read 1 Corinthians 14:26–40 out loud at least once.
—Read 1 Corinthians 14:26–40 at least once silently to yourself. Read it very slowly, allowing time for each word and phrase to resonate.

REFLECT

A Thought of Reflection

There are several passages in 1 Corinthians where the historical and cultural context is difficult to understand fully, thus it is equally hard to choose a definitive interpretation. This is one of them. Despite some differences in the specifics of passages like this one, we do know that Paul is unwaveringly calling the church to act according to love and the way of the cross rather than in their own interest.

What is clear in this passage is that Paul wants them to institute a bit of order into their gatherings. The Spirit doesn't work only through spontaneity. Although there can be abuses in extreme forms of order that drift into control and thinking everything must be "perfect" or "excellent," he encourages them to have the sort of order that shows deference and respect and allows everyone to participate equally so that it builds up the body. The number of speakers should be limited, orderly, and with discernment. It is not a free-for-all. If there is no interpreter or if someone else would like to speak, the one speaking should keep silent. This is an act of love.

The question comes in whether verses 34–38 are another example of calling someone to silence for speaking inappropriately and out of order, in this case women, or if some of the Corinthian men were acting like the surrounding cultures and demanding that the women not speak. While there are many interpretations and opinions, the most consistent contextually seems to be the latter. Verses 34–35, then, would be yet another of the many times in this letter where Paul quotes the Corinthians before refuting their faulty reasoning. That would help explain the reference to "the law." There is nothing in the Old Testament law like this, but both the Jewish Mishnah and Roman law had elements of this nature. Bolstering this view is that verse 36 begins with an onomatopoeia, *eta*, which is untranslated in the NIV. The closest English translation would be "pffft," although some translators have supplied "What?!" or "Bunk!" It is a term of refutation. Also, the phrase, "are you the only people" in Greek is written in the masculine, indicating it addresses men only. In this scenario, Paul calls them to not attempt to put women in the place of inferiority but to let them speak (as he has already described in 11:5). If it is the other scenario, then Paul is recommending that control and order for the benefit of the body be the rule. Whatever the specifics, Paul wants everything to be done in "a fitting and orderly way" that reflects a love for one another.

Preparation for Reflection

1. Why is order in gatherings so important to Paul?

2. How do self-control and concern for others and the good of the body factor into Paul's directions in this passage?

3. If speaking in languages was so open to misuse, why do you think Paul did not just forbid the practice?

RECITE

Take 2–3 minutes to meditate on your own on the phrase, "Everything should be done in a fitting and orderly way." Listen for the Spirit to reveal new insights of understanding and application of this phrase to your life.

RESPOND

As you move into a time of prayer, focus on the things you normally pray for but today take some time to pray:

- that worship gatherings in your church will be encouraging and unifying.

- for energy and encouragement for those who work hard to plan and prepare for worship gatherings.

- that God will work through your worship gatherings to prepare each person to live out their kingdom citizenship in their respective contexts through the remainder of the week.

THE REMAINDER OF THE WEEK

 Questions for Reflection

- What can I do specifically to show appreciation to someone who works hard each week to help keep order in worship gatherings?

- Who can I invite this week to either a small group meeting or a large worship gathering?

Application

- What is an application that you take away from this section for your faith community?

- What is the personal application that you take away from this section?

Further Study (Optional)

- Read the following article about women remaining silent in the church: "1 Corinthians 14:33b–38 as a Pauline Quotation-Refutation Device," (CBE International).

https://www.cbeinternational.org/resource/1-corinthians-1433b-38-pauline-quotation-refutation-device/

1 CORINTHIANS 15:1–11

DAY 33

"He appeared to Cephas; and after that to the twelve." So, if you disbelieve one witness, you have twelve witnesses. "Then he was seen by more than five hundred people at once"—if they disbelieve the twelve, then listen to the five hundred. "After that, he was seen by James," his own brother and the first overseer of [Jerusalem]. Since so noteworthy a bishop was privileged to see the risen Christ, along with the other disciples, do not disbelieve. But you may say that his brother was a biased witness. So, then he continues: "He was seen by me." But who am I? I am Paul, his enemy! "I was formerly a persecutor" but now preach the good news of the resurrection.

—Cyril of Jerusalem, 4th century AD

READ

—Read 1 Corinthians 15:1–11 out loud at least once.
—Read 1 Corinthians 15:1–11 at least once silently to yourself. Read it very slowly, allowing time for each word and phrase to resonate.

REFLECT

A Thought of Reflection

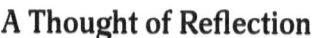

Before we can fully appreciate Paul's intentions in 1 Corinthians 15, we must be clear on two things. The first is that his turn to resurrection is not an abrupt departure from the rest of the letter if we can follow his thinking. For Paul, being in Christ meant to be people of the resurrection. That was the great hope of the Christian faith. It is where the story has been heading all along. One day God will restore his creation, transform his people through resurrection, and live with them in his presence. The resurrection and the new creation are virtually synonymous terms. So everything Paul has been calling the Corinthians to embody is informed by the resurrection age. They are to live out that reality in the present age. So, to deny the physical resurrection was to fundamentally deny their own identity.

The second important element that we must be clear on is the general Greco-Roman beliefs on the body and resurrection. This is the backdrop for much of Paul's comments, as it appears that, once again, the Corinthians were relying on the culture around them to inform their mindsets and identities. Although there were variations, the typical cultural understanding was that the physical realm was tainted and inferior to the spiritual realm. The great hope for them was to die and have the soul released from the body to go into their version of the afterlife. The idea of a physical resurrection was not only laughable to the Greco-Romans but was wholly undesirable. Thus, it would have been something that the Corinthians were likely uncomfortable with at the start and quick to refashion according to their cultural sensibilities. But if the resurrection is removed or altered to fit their cultural background, then the whole new-creation life to which they are called falls apart. The pillar for it all is that Jesus physically died and physically walked out of death (and there are many witnesses they can consult). The resurrection of Christ in the past and the resurrection of his people in the future are the foundation of our faith, our hope, and our love.

Before we dismiss this as an issue only in first-century Corinth, read again about their cultural beliefs that the goal after death was for the soul to escape the body and live in a "spiritual" disembodied state in the afterlife. Paul expressly rejects that as a denial of the resurrection. Is it possible that we have been more impacted by Greek philosophers and Western thinking in contemporary Christianity than we realize?

Preparation for Reflection

1. What are the connections between physical resurrection and the rest of Paul's letter?

2. Why is the physical resurrection of Jesus so important to Paul?

3. Why do you think the physical resurrection of believers is so important to Paul?

RECITE

Take 2–3 minutes to meditate on your own on the phrase, "By this gospel you are saved." Listen for the Spirit to reveal new insights of understanding and application of this phrase to your life.

RESPOND

As you move into a time of prayer, focus on the things you normally pray for but today take some time to pray:

- and thank God that Jesus defeated death and shared his victory with us.

- and thank God for forgiving us our sins.

- and thank God that we will one day be resurrected physically and dwell in his presence.

THE REMAINDER OF THE WEEK

Questions for Reflection

- What would it look like to live every facet of my life in light of the resurrection of the saints?

- Do I believe in physical resurrection, or have I been somewhat influenced by Greek philosophy and belief in the soul escaping the body?

Application

- What is an application that you take away from this section for your faith community?

- How can you apply this to your personal life?

Further Study (Optional)

- Read the following article about the fourth-century Christian views of the resurrection: Chris De Wet, "John Chrysostom's Exegesis on the Resurrection in 1 Corinthians 15," PDF (Academia.edu).

https://www.academia.edu/3821535/John_Chrysostoms_Exegesis_on_the_Resurrection_in_1_Corinthians_15

1 CORINTHIANS 15:12-19

DAY 34

It is clear that the souls of his disciples also (upon whose account the Lord underwent these things) will go away into the invisible place allotted to them by God. And they will remain there until the resurrection awaiting that event. Then receiving their bodies and rising in their entirety (that is bodily), just as the Lord arose, they will come in that manner into the presence of God.

—Irenaeus, 2nd century AD

READ

—Read 1 Corinthians 15:12–19 out loud at least once.
—Read 1 Corinthians 15:12–19 at least once silently to yourself. Read it very slowly, allowing time for each word and phrase to resonate.

REFLECT

A Thought of Reflection

Time and again the Corinthians had been guilty of allowing their culture to take the leash and lead them, and Paul patiently points out the problem in each situation. But in doing so when it comes to their understanding of resurrection, this is a full-out disaster. If they don't comprehend the implications of the resurrection of Christ and their own future resurrection, then the whole project is lost. There is simply no point in maintaining faith at all. Without the resurrection, there is no faith. That is clear. But it is also true that if they twist what resurrection is, they will wind up twisting the expression of their faith. In the first half of this chapter, Paul clarifies the necessity of believing in the physical resurrection of Christ, then he moves on to explain their coming resurrection and why correctly understanding that matters.

It appears that some were denying the possibility of physical resurrection, likely by claiming it to be a spiritual stage that had already happened in the life of a believer. Others were filling the vessel of resurrection with ideas that came from Plato and Greek philosophy, espousing that it took place when the soul escaped the body at death and went into a shadowy spiritual realm. But if either of those is true, then Christ did not physically resurrect. And this changes everything, says Paul. He describes five massive implications. The first is that preaching is profitless. The second is that faith is futile. The third is that Jesus' messengers have misinformed them with a lie. The fourth is that sin is sovereign, and they have not been freed. The fifth is that death still has dominion, and those who have passed already are gone eternally.

If the hope of the Christian faith does not end in physical resurrection and the restoration of the cosmos to the new creation, then we are to be pitied more than anyone else on earth. The way of the cross is what happens when the followers of Jesus live the life of the new creation while still in the present age. It is a life of self-denial, giving up our rights and sacrificing for the benefit of others. If Jesus didn't walk out of the grave and if we will not one day be with him in the new creation, then all of that is bunk, and we might as well go home. This all means that we should not be fuzzy on the biblical teaching of the resurrection. Understanding it and allowing it to inform how we live now is essential.

Preparation for Reflection

1. What does it tell us about how confident Paul was that Jesus was resurrected and that he was willing to pin the entirety of the Christian faith on whether it happened?

2. Why were the resurrection of Christ and the hope of the resurrection of believers so important in Paul's mind?

3. If the concept of resurrection was so important to Paul and the proper framing of our faith, do we consider it enough and understand it well enough in today's Christianity?

RECITE

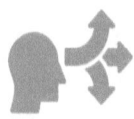 Take 2–3 minutes to meditate on your own on the phrase, "If only for this life we have hope in Christ, we are of all people most to be pitied." Listen for the Spirit to reveal new insights of understanding and application of this phrase to your life.

RESPOND

As you move into a time of prayer, focus on the things you normally pray for but today take some time to pray:

• for a deeper understanding of the importance of the resurrection of Christ.

• for a deeper understanding of the importance of the resurrection of those in Christ.

• that God will encourage your church and give you the resolve to put in the work to understand those concepts in a better way.

THE REMAINDER OF THE WEEK

Questions for Reflection

• How important a role does the resurrection of the believers play in my daily life?

• What can I do to learn more about the importance of resurrection?

Application

• What is an application that you take away from this section for your faith community?

• What is the personal application that you take away from this section?

Further Study (Optional)

• Watch the following video of N. T. Wright speaking on the importance of the resurrection: (3396) Dr. N. T. Wright, "Did Jesus Really Rise from the Dead?" (YouTube).

https://www.youtube.com/watch?v=KnkNKIJ_dnw

1 CORINTHIANS 15:20-28

DAY 35

We believe that there will be a resurrection of bodies after the consummation of all things.

—Tatian, 2nd century AD

READ

—Read 1 Corinthians 15:20–28 out loud at least once.

—Read 1 Corinthians 15:20–28 at least once silently to yourself. Read it very slowly, allowing time for each word and phrase to resonate.

REFLECT

A Thought of Reflection

At the heart of this section is the concept of order. The word "order" doesn't directly appear in the NIV, but this is what Paul is speaking of in this passage, connecting it with the idea of order back in chapter 14. Two aspects regarding order come to the forefront here. The first is the timeline of resurrection itself. The people of Israel were awaiting the resurrection of the righteous, but they believed it would be at the end of time. They knew it would happen but were unclear exactly how it would come about. But Jesus' resurrection had made it clear to Paul that it had happened in the middle of the present age. It had not happened how or when he had imagined it. This meant that the coming of God's kingdom and the resurrection were taking place in two stages. Christ's resurrection was the firstfruits, meaning the sample and guarantee of the coming resurrection of those in him. He has defeated the powers and authorities and all that has corrupted and defaced God's creation, but that victory has yet to be fully implemented. One day, death will be completely defeated, and God will be fully and completely present and known in his creation.

And that leads to the second topic of order that Paul addresses here. In Jesus' victory, the cosmos will be put back into its intended order. And part of that order is the status of Jesus. He and the

Father are one, but he is the Father's only and true Son. Rather than striving for a position and status that are not his, Jesus will subject his authority to God the Father.

Making sense of this in *1 Corinthians* in his For Everyone Bible Study Guides, N. T. Wright says, "Into this picture of a world put back to rights, Paul has woven several strands taken from the Old Testament. He quotes two psalms that were often used in the church to speak of Jesus' messianic rule. Psalm 110...is about the king whom God will place at his right hand until all his enemies are brought into subjection. This, Paul declares, is now being fulfilled in Jesus. Psalm 8...belongs closely with this, speaking of God 'putting all things into order under his feet.' But instead of talking about the Messiah...[it] talks about the human being. This task of being under God and over the world is not just the task of the Messiah; it's what God had in mind from the very start when he created humans in his own image." This was always God's plan to bring the world back to order and establish his reign.

Resurrection is not a peripheral issue. It is the defining goal of the new humanity in Christ that represents order both in the present age and in the age to come. Without it, there is no proper identity in the present and no hope for the future.

Preparation for Reflection

1. Firstfruits in Israel was the practice of taking a small portion of a crop before the rest. It served as a sample of the crop as well as a guarantee that the rest of the crop was good and would be reaped soon. Why does Paul use that as a metaphor for the resurrection of Christ?

2. Christians today often relativize the impact of death by focusing on going to heaven right after death. Yet Paul is clear here that death will not be destroyed fully until Christ returns. What is the significance of Paul's timeline, so to speak, for the destruction of death?

3. Given the context of this letter, why do you think Paul may have emphasized that Christ would not hold tightly to his kingship over creation but would willingly give it up to the Father one day?

RECITE

Take 2–3 minutes to meditate on your own on the phrase, "so that God may be all in all." Listen for the Spirit to reveal new insights of understanding and application of this phrase to your life.

RESPOND

As you move into a time of prayer, focus on the things you normally pray for but today take some time to pray:

- for the friends and family of those you knew who have passed away recently.

- that the church will continue to anticipate and proclaim Christ's defeat of the powers and authorities by living according to the reality and values of the new creation.

- specifically for three people who are not in Christ currently and petition God to move in their lives in a powerful way to bring them to submit to Jesus as their King.

THE REMAINDER OF THE WEEK

Questions for Reflection

- Does your life demonstrate that Jesus is King?
- What can I do today to help the three people from my prayer time come to know Jesus as King?

Application

- How can you apply these lessons to your church?
- How can you apply these lessons to your own life?

Further Study (Optional)

- Read the article about the powers and authorities in 1 Cor. 15: "Gentile Gods at the Eschaton: A Reconsideration of Paul's 'Principalities and Powers' in 1 Corinthians 15" (*Journal of Biblical Literature*, Scholarly Publishing Collective).

https://scholarlypublishingcollective.org/sblpress/jbl/article-abstract/136/3/727/179308/Gentile-Gods-at-the-Eschaton-A-Reconsideration-of?redirectedFrom=fulltext

1 CORINTHIANS 15:29-34

If all hope of the resurrection is lost, let us eat and drink and lose not the enjoyment of the things present, for we have none to come.... The Epicureans say they are followers of pleasure because death means nothing to them. After all, that which is dissolved has no feeling, and that which has no feeling means nothing to us. Thus, they show that they are living only carnally, not spiritually. They do not discharge the duty of the soul but only of the flesh. They think that all life's duty is ended with the separation of the soul and body.

—Ambrose, 4th century AD

READ

—Read 1 Corinthians 15:29–34 out loud at least once.

—Read 1 Corinthians 15:29–34 at least once silently to yourself. Read it very slowly, allowing time for each word and phrase to resonate.

REFLECT

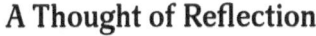

A Thought of Reflection

Verse 29 has sparked confusion among Christians for centuries, resulting in many unsubstantiated theories that could somehow explain this strange reference to what appears to be a puzzling practice in Corinth in the first century. The most plausible and contextually consistent explanation for this passage, however, is not strange at all. Paul has repeatedly laid out logical inconsistencies for a Christian who denies the physical resurrection. Here he throws out one more.

It helps to identify how Paul often described his ministry as an apostle. The apostles, he says, are like those being led to their deaths at the end of a triumphal procession (1 Cor. 4:9; 2 Cor. 2:14–16). He was crucified with Christ and no longer lives for himself (Gal. 2:20). This was not just a one-time event. Rather, he carries around in his body the death of Jesus and is being given over to death, which is at work in him every day (2 Cor. 4:10–12). His way of life was a constant expression of the way of the cross (2 Cor. 6:4–10; 2 Cor. 11:23–29). Christians, and especially Christian leaders, had died to themselves and were the walking dead. Yet the Corinthians were factionalizing over which leader they identified with, having been baptized on account of their ministry (1 Cor. 1:12–17). Why would they be baptized "for" or "on account of" these "dead" men? Why respond to their ministry and inappropriately seek status based on who baptized you if there is no resurrection? If there is no resurrection, then they are truly just dead men walking with no hope and should be pitied. Why would Paul constantly risk his own life? Why would he face the persecution he did in places like Ephesus? What would be the point of following someone who has pinned their entire life on the hope of the resurrection if there is no such thing?

Anthony Thiselton, in his *1 Corinthians* commentary, asserts that "bad company" referred to their in-group of influence. Paul's point, then, was that they were being influenced by the wrong cultural forces. Their rejection of resurrection was feeding their dangerous appetite for the wrong influences and this, in turn, was leading them directly away from the way of the cross.

Preparation for Reflection

1. Why do you think Paul so frequently compared the life of a Christian to death? What are some of the teachings of Jesus that led him to believe this was the case?

2. What do you think Paul was referring to when he spoke about those being baptized for the dead?

3. The Corinthians seemed to resist anything that called them to give up their rights, lower their status or privilege, and embrace the way of the cross and dying to self. Do you see any examples of that same instinct in today's church? What are some specific examples?

RECITE

Take 2–3 minutes to meditate on your own on the phrase, "I face death every day." Listen for the Spirit to reveal new insights of understanding and application of this phrase to your life.

RESPOND

As you move into a time of prayer, focus on the things you normally pray for but today take some time to pray:

- that the brothers and sisters in your church, including you, will be willing to fully embrace the life of dying to self and not shrink back from it.

- that God will show you specific opportunities to die to yourself.

- for those who have been influenced by the wrong in-group, keeping Matthew 7:1–6 in mind as you pray.

THE REMAINDER OF THE WEEK

Questions for Reflection

- What are some of the wrong in-groups that might influence my life?

- Am I willing to die to myself each day for the sake of the gospel?

Application

- What is an application that you take away from this section for your faith community?

- What is the personal application that you take away from this section?

Further Study (Optional)

- Read the following article about baptism for the dead: "'Baptized on Account of the Dead': The Meaning of 1 Corinthians 15:29 in Its Context" (*Journal of Biblical Literature*, Scholarly Publishing Collective).

https://scholarlypublishingcollective.org/sblpress/jbl/article-abstract/116/3/487/182961/Baptized-on-Account-of-the-Dead-The-Meaning-of-1?redirectedFrom=fulltext

1 CORINTHIANS 15:35-49

DAY 37

Why does Paul argue like this, instead of simply referring his hearers to the power of God as he does elsewhere? Here he is dealing with people who do not believe in what he is saying, so he gives them reasons for it.

—Chrysostom, 4th century AD

READ

—Read 1 Corinthians 15:35–49 out loud at least once.
—Read 1 Corinthians 15:35–49 at least once silently to yourself. Read it very slowly, allowing time for each word and phrase to resonate.

REFLECT

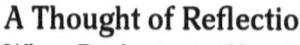

A Thought of Reflection

When Paul retorts "How foolish!" or "That is nonsense," he is not referring to the act of them asking questions. What is nonsense is the implication that resurrection cannot be, simply because they cannot conceive of how it would work. Their questions are the fruit of a mind that rejects what God is doing, namely resurrection, because it cannot comprehend how he would do it, that is, what the resurrection body could be. Paul responds by arguing that nature provides analogies and pictures of the kind of thing that resurrection could be. It is like a seed that flowers into a fuller expression of itself. And there are numerous examples of similar things that are different in their mode of existence. While the present body and the resurrection body are similar, perhaps more so than we may realize, there will be important differences.

If we fail to understand how Paul uses the terms "natural" and "spiritual," we can easily get off track in this passage and think he is saying something quite different from what he intended. These do not refer to the material substance of the body but rather to what animates it. The natural body is animated by our desires and temptations. The spiritual body is animated by God's nature and Spirit. The present human body, of which Adam is the prototype or representative, is constantly in a state of decay. It is perishable. The resurrection body will be like these bodies but is imperishable, or a reversal of decay. The present body is fallen and stuck in dishonor. The resurrection body is raised in its fullest expression and mode, carrying the full majesty of potential human existence. In other words, the present body is animated by human nature and desires. It is prone to sinful choices. The resurrection body will be transformed. But for Paul, the problem is not skin, as we might suppose. It is sin. The resurrection body will be animated by the desires and power of the Spirit. It will not be prone to sin. Can you imagine waking each morning and not being filled with selfish and sinful desires? That is the reality of the resurrection body. No longer will we represent our own will, but we will fully reflect the will and image of the creator God.

But if there is no resurrection of the physical body, Paul implies, then there is no hope of this. There can be no transformation. There will be no defeat of death. To float away in a form more like Casper the friendly ghost is not a defeat of death. It is not the resurrection body that Jesus displayed. That type of existence does not contain the power and glory of God in its fullness.

Preparation for Reflection

1. What is your response when the Bible promises things or makes claims, and you cannot fathom how that could be? Is it faith or skepticism?

2. According to Paul, what is the difference between the physical and spiritual body?

3. How do common contemporary misunderstandings of what happens when we die and the resurrection compare to what the Corinthians thought? How do they differ?

RECITE

Take 2–3 minutes to meditate on your own on the phrase, "We shall bear the image of the heavenly man." Listen for the Spirit to reveal new insights of understanding and application of this phrase to your life.

RESPOND

As you move into a time of prayer, focus on the things you normally pray for but today take some time to pray:

- for disciples who struggle in understanding or in accepting aspects of God's word.

- for the time of the resurrection to come quickly but also for patience if it doesn't.

- and thank God that he will one day transform our bodies into the glory of a resurrection body animated by his Spirit.

THE REMAINDER OF THE WEEK

Questions for Reflection

- What are some of the cultural assumptions and structures that can work their way into the life of the church that I may have continued to accept without examination?

- Are there any ways in which I have contributed to division in the body of Christ?

Application

- How do I respond when I find things in God's word that I do not understand?

- Do I live my life as though the physical resurrection and restoration of creation are more determinative of my actions than the values of the present age?

Further Study (Optional)

- Read the following article about Paul's cultural understanding of resurrection: "Resurrection in Paganism and the Question of an Empty Tomb in 1 Corinthians 15" in *New Testament Studies* (Cambridge Core).

https://www.cambridge.org/core/journals/new-testament-studies/article/resurrection-in-paganism-and-the-question-of-an-empty-tomb-in-1-corinthians-15/EF4DE640BE9104A454C7847ECF899313

1 CORINTHIANS 15:50-58

"Flesh and blood cannot inherit the kingdom of God." This is put forward by all the heretics in support of their folly [i.e., their denial of the resurrection of the body]. They do this to try to annoy us and to point out that the handiwork of God [i.e., the flesh] is not saved.... However, by "flesh and blood," Paul refers to all of those (as many as there are) who do not have that [Spirit] which saves and forms us into life. These are the ones who do not have the Spirit of God in themselves. For that reason, men of this mold are spoken of by the Lord as "dead." For he says, "Let the dead bury their dead."

—Irenaeus, 2nd century AD

READ

—Read 1 Corinthians 15:50–58 out loud at least once.
—Read 1 Corinthians 15:50–58 at least once silently to yourself. Read it very slowly, allowing time for each word and phrase to resonate.

REFLECT

A Thought of Reflection

Before clarifying one more important aspect of resurrection, Paul takes a moment to center the Corinthians on who they are becoming as kingdom people. Flesh and blood, he says, cannot inherit the kingdom. It becomes clear in this verse and by the context of what he has just stated in verses 45–49 that he is not talking about a material existence versus a nonmaterial state but about what animates us. When Jesus appeared to the disciples following his resurrection, he assured them that he was not a ghost but was flesh and bone (Luke 24:39). For Paul, flesh and blood is a metaphor for a life not committed to being different (holy). They cannot have the world be their determining in-group and still expect to inherit the kingdom of God.

His last flourish revolves around transformation. One day Christ will return. There will be no warnings or signs. It will simply come. And when it does, those physically alive at that moment will be transformed and those who have died will be raised to life. The great enemy of humanity, death, will be defeated once and for all. It is at this time that death will lose its sting.

Interestingly, there have been many non-Christians who have faced death with no concern or fear. Yet in Gethsemane Jesus wrestled in horror with the oncoming specter of death. He asked God to remove that cup from him but was faithful when he didn't. Anthony Thiselton says this is because Jesus faced death as "God-forsakenness." It is a very real enemy. Death is not part of God's ultimate desire for his creation. And Jesus walked into the terror of death, but then punched a hole and walked out the other side. So we need not pretend or act on the illusion that death is not to be feared. Because of Christ, Thiselton says, we can now recognize that death is terrible but also that it holds no ultimate horror.

If we truly understand the implications of resurrection, it reorders everything in our lives. Resurrection is a greater reality than physical death. That means we should live and operate as beings who are destined to rise again one day fully and completely, not just in a shadowy soulish form. We need not operate as though death has the final word and must be avoided at all costs. So, Paul reminds them, all the effort and labor they have put in to be all things to all people, to raise the marginalized, to give up their rights, and to embody the new creation is not in vain.

Preparation for Reflection

1. Does death still hold terrors for you to the degree that it can dictate some of your decisions or actions more than the reality of resurrection?

2. In your own words, what does Paul mean when he says that flesh and blood cannot inherit the kingdom of God?

3. What does Paul mean when he says that your labor in the Lord is not in vain?

RECITE

Take 2–3 minutes to meditate on your own on the phrase, "Where, O death is your victory?" Listen for the Spirit to reveal new insights of understanding and application of this phrase to your life.

RESPOND

As you move into a time of prayer, focus on the things you normally pray for but today take some time to pray:

- for God's comfort to rest on those who have recently experienced the death of a loved one.

- that God will continue to give you insight into what it means to live with resurrection as a greater reality than physical death.

- that the brothers and sisters in your church and your small group will stand firm to the end.

THE REMAINDER OF THE WEEK

Questions for Reflection

- Do I give myself fully to the work of the Lord and embody the new creation?

- How do I respond if I ever get discouraged and start to feel that my labor in the Lord is in vain?

Application

- What is an application that you take away from this section for your faith community?

- What is the personal application that you take away from this section?

Further Study (Optional)

- Read N. T. Wright's book, *Surprised by Hope: Rethinking Heaven, the Resurrection, and the Mission of the Church* (Amazon.com).

https://www.amazon.com/Surprised-Hope-Rethinking-Resurrection-Mission/dp/0061551821/ref=tmm_hrd_swatch_0?_encoding=UTF8&qid=1666882739&sr=8-1

1 CORINTHIANS 16:1-12

This collection was doubly beneficial because it helped the saints mentioned above and also the poor people who were in the church.

—Chrysostom, 4th century AD

READ

—Read 1 Corinthians 16:1–12 out loud at least once.
—Read 1 Corinthians 16:1–12 at least once silently to yourself. Read it very slowly, allowing time for each word and phrase to resonate.

REFLECT

A Thought of Reflection

It is easy to look at the collection that Paul mentions as something simply tacked onto the end of his letter, almost like the closing announcements in a church gathering. But this collection was a central feature of Paul's ministry. He mentions it in several of his letters to churches (Rom. 15:25–28; 1 Cor. 16:1–4; 2 Cor. 8:1–9:15; Gal. 2:10) and saw it as the embodiment of who the churches were and what they were becoming as the image-bearers of the new creation. This collection was unique in the ancient world. There were various forms of benefaction, but nothing like a collection from a broad base of people that would be distributed to a large group. There was simply no precedent for such a thing. The outside world would have viewed it quite suspiciously. And this was quite the point for Paul. Who would do such a thing? Who would live like this? Only a group of people who had completely abandoned the wisdom of the world and the values of the present age, only a new-creation people. Because of a severe famine and other unknown factors, it seems that the disciples in Jerusalem were in dire need. Paul saw this as an opportunity to demonstrate giving up one's rights and possessions for the benefit of their brothers and sisters in need. It was sacrificial. It was love. It was family. It was selfless. It was the way of the cross. It was everything they should strive to be.

This was no tithe or regular collection to run the affairs of the church. This was living out the reality of a new-creation economy. It was creating a new society where there was no lack and no surplus. If they were one people, then showing this kind of love and concern for others whom they had never met was essential. They were all in this together.

The life of the new creation was reflected in the interweaving of their relationships as well. Traveling teachers in the ancient world typically went from town to town to amass followers, which would increase their status and prestige. It was unheard-of to go to a town for the benefit of others or to simply encourage and help them. But this is precisely what we see here. Decisions were considered, itineraries were set, and visits were made, all based on love for others. This is part of what it looked like to escape the status games of the culture and the pursuit of superiority and advantage over others. This is what following Jesus looked like in the real world.

Preparation for Reflection

1. Why was the collection for Jerusalem so important to Paul?

2. Why do you think Paul wanted each Gentile church to send a representative with their collection to Jerusalem rather than just sending the money?

3. Why did Paul not want to see them right at that time? What does that tell us about how he felt about them?

RECITE

Take 2–3 minutes to meditate on your own on the phrase, "See to it that he has nothing to fear while he is with you." Listen for the Spirit to reveal new insights of understanding and application of this phrase to your Christian walk.

RESPOND

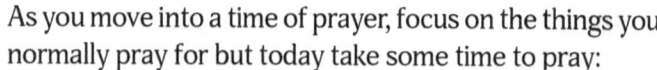

As you move into a time of prayer, focus on the things you normally pray for but today take some time to pray:

    • for your church to continue to participate with all its heart in opportunities to help brothers and sisters in need.

• that God will inspire and equip your church to love one another in tangible and creative ways that demonstrate the arrival of the new creation.

• for those who regularly travel to teach, encourage, or strengthen other congregations. Pray that they may be led by the Spirit, that they may be effective, and that they may have the energy and courage to complete their tasks.

THE REMAINDER OF THE WEEK

Questions for Reflection

• Are there ways in which I can help brothers and sisters in need that I have not yet engaged in?

• What can I do to support the ministry of those who are called to travel to encourage and strengthen other churches?

Application

• What is an application that you take away from this section for your faith community?

• What is the personal application that you take away from this section?

Further Study (Optional)

• Read the following article about Paul's collection for the Jerusalem church: "The leadership challenges of Paul's collection for the saints in Jerusalem," PDF (scielo.org.za).

http://www.scielo.org.za/pdf/vee/v38n1/41.pdf

1 CORINTHIANS 16:13-24

If love had been present, the Corinthians would not have been puffed up, they would not have divided into factions, they would not have gone to law before heathens, or indeed at all. If there had been love in the church, that notorious person would not have taken his father's wife, they would not have looked down on their weaker brethren, and they would not have boasted about their spiritual gifts.

—Chrysostom, 4th century AD

READ

—Read 1 Corinthians 16:13–24 out loud at least once.
—Read 1 Corinthians 16:13–24 at least once silently to yourself. Read it very slowly, allowing time for each word and phrase to resonate.

REFLECT

A Thought of Reflection

What should the Corinthians be on guard against? What does it look like to stand firm in the faith? What does it mean to be courageous? How should they be strong? How would they go about doing everything in love? In one sense, Paul has been answering those questions all along. They should resist the wisdom of their culture and age. Near the onset of this letter, Paul spoke of the cross of Christ (1 Cor. 1:23; 2:2), and near the end, of the resurrection (1 Cor. 15:1–58). It is those two events that have broken a hole into the present age, allowing the new creation to come rushing in through the work of the Spirit. It is the cross and the empty tomb that have turned the wisdom of the world upside down. It is to this life of new creation that Paul has called them.

But in another sense, Paul will give them one last tangible example of what being on guard against the wisdom of the world, standing firm in the faith, living strongly and courageously, and acting in love looks like: It looks like the household of Stephanas.

They were very likely among the strong and high-status groups. The cultural expectation was for elites to be served and attended to by those of lower status. Yet Stephanas' household was the reverse of that. They devoted themselves to serving the Lord's people. This is what the way of the cross looks like. This is what alert, firm, strong, courageous love looks like. They served others. They flipped the cultural script and eschewed the wisdom of the world. Rather than leaders who are puffed up, boast about their status, and use others to gain privilege for themselves, these are the kind of leaders that they should submit to and trust. With that final reminder, Paul sends warm family greetings, ensures that he has written the final salutation with his own hand, and ends with the blessings of Christ.

As we come to the end of our journey through 1 Corinthians, Paul's words in verse 13 are a fitting place to end. We have seen what these exhortations meant in the context of the first-century world. Now it is up to us to take that and learn from it. It is our task to allow that information to disciple us and continue the process of becoming the people of the new creation.

Preparation for Reflection

1. In the context of this letter, what might Paul mean specifically by urging them to be on their guard?

2. Given the cultural and historical context, what do you think might have been some of the biggest obstacles for the Corinthians that caused Paul to remind them to stand firm in the faith and be courageous?

3. Why did Paul praise the household of Stephanas? In calling them to submit to these kinds of leaders, what is Paul subtly implying about other leaders?

RECITE

Take 2–3 minutes to meditate on your own on the phrase, "Do everything in love." Listen for the Spirit to reveal new insights of understanding and application of this phrase to your Christian walk.

RESPOND

As you move into a time of prayer, focus on the things you normally pray for but today take some time to pray:

- for your church to be on its guard against worldly wisdom and inappropriate cultural influence.

- for your church to stand firm in the faith and be courageous and strong.

- for your church to do everything in love.

THE REMAINDER OF THE WEEK

Questions for Reflection

- How is the Spirit calling me to be on my guard against cultural influences?

- Do I do everything in love? If not, how can I grow in that?

Application

- What is an application that you take away from this section for your faith community?

- What is the personal application that you take away from this section?

Further Study (Optional)

- Read the following article about Stephanas and Paul's redefinition of group dynamics: (4) Jack Barentsen, "Stephanas as Model Leader: A Social Identity Perspective on Community and Leadership (Mis)formation in Corinth" (Academia.edu)..

https://www.academia.edu/en/9667758/Stephanas_as_Model_Leader_A_Social_Identity_Perspective_on_Community_and_Leadership_Mis_formation_in_Corinth

Books for Christian Growth from Illumination Publishers

Apologetics

Compelling Evidence for God and the Bible—Truth in an Age of Doubt, by Douglas Jacoby.
Field Manual for Christian Apologetics, by John M. Oakes.
Is There a God—Questions and Answers about Science and the Bible, by John M. Oakes.
Mormonism—What Do the Evidence and Testimony Reveal? by John M. Oakes.
Reasons for Belief-A Handbook of Christian Evidence, by John M. Oakes.
That You May Believe—Reflections on Science and Jesus, by John Oakes/David Eastman.
The Resurrection: A Historical Analysis, by C. Foster Stanback.
When God Is Silent—The Problem of Human Suffering, by Douglas Jacoby.

Bible Basics

A Disciple's Handbook—Third Edition, Tom A. Jones, Editor.
A Quick Overview of the Bible, by Douglas Jacoby.
Be Still, My Soul—A Practical Guide to a Deeper Relationship with God, by Sam Laing.
From Shadow to Reality—Relationship of the Old & New Testament, by John M. Oakes.
Getting the Most from the Bible, Second Edition, by G. Steve Kinnard.
Letters to New Disciples—Practical Advice for New Followers of Jesus, by Tom A. Jones.
The Baptized Life—The Lifelong Meaning of Immersion into Christ, by Tom A. Jones.
The Lion Never Sleeps—Preparing Those You Love for Satan's Attacks, by Mike Taliaferro.
The New Christian's Field Guide, Joseph Dindinger, Editor.
Thirty Days at the Foot of the Cross, Tom and Sheila Jones, Editors.

Christian Living

According to Your Faith—The Awesome Power of Belief in God, by Richard Alawaye.
But What About Your Anger—A Biblical Guide to Managing Your Anger, by Lee Boger.
Caring Beyond the Margins—Understanding Homosexuality, by Guy Hammond.
Free Your Mind—40 Days to Greater Peace, Hope, and Joy, by Sam Laing.
Golden Rule Membership—What God Expects of Every Disciple, by John M. Oakes.
Jesus and the Poor—Embracing the Ministry of Jesus, by G. Steve Kinnard.
How to Be a Missionary in Your Hometown, by Joel Nagel.
Like a Tree Planted by Streams of Water—Personal Spiritual Growth, by G. Steve Kinnard.
Love One Another—Importance & Power of Christian Relationships, by Gordon Ferguson.
One Another—Transformational Relationships, by Tom A. Jones and Steve Brown.
Prepared to Answer—Restoring Truth in an Age of Relativism, by Gordon Ferguson.
Repentance—A Cosmic Shift of Mind & Heart, by Edward J. Anton.
Strong in the Grace—Reclaiming the Heart of the Gospel, by Tom A. Jones.
Tempt-Away: How to Defeat Temptation in Under 60 Seconds, by Guy Hammond.
The Guilty Soul's Guide to Grace—Freedom in Christ, by Sam Laing.
The Power of Discipling, by Gordon Ferguson.
The Prideful Soul's Guide to Humility, by Tom A. Jones and Michael Fontenot.
The Way of the Heart—Spiritual Living in a Legalistic World, by G. Steve Kinnard.
The Way of the Heart of Jesus—Prayer, Fasting, Bible Study, by G. Steve Kinnard.
Till the Nets Are Full—An Evangelism Handbook for the 21st Century, by Douglas Jacoby.
Walking the Way of the Heart—Lessons for Spiritual Living, by G. Steve Kinnard.
When God Is Silent—The Problem of Human Suffering, by Douglas Jacoby.
Values and Habits of Spiritual Growth, by Bryan Gray.

All Available at www.ipibooks.com

Deeper Study

A Women's Ministry Handbook, by Jennifer Lambert and Kay McKean.

After the Storm—Hope & Healing From Ezra—Nehemiah, by Rolan Dia Monje.

Aliens and Strangers—The Life and Letters of Peter, by Brett Kreider.

Crossing the Line: Culture, Race, and Kingdom, by Michael Burns.

Daniel—Prophet to the Nations, by John M. Oakes.

Exodus—Making Israel's Journey Your Own, by Rolan Dia Monje.

Exodus—Night of Redemption, by Douglas Jacoby.

Finish Strong—The Message of Haggai, Zechariah, and Malachi, by Rolan Dia Monje.

In Remembrance of Me—Understanding the Lord's Supper, by Andrew C. Fleming.

In the Middle of It!—Tools to Help Preteen and Young Teen Leaders, by Jeff Rorabaugh.

Into the Psalms—Verses for the Heart, Music for the Soul, by Rolan Dia Monje.

King Jesus—A Survey of the Life of Jesus the Messiah, by G. Steve Kinnard.

Jesus Unequaled—An Exposition of Colossians, by G. Steve Kinnard.

Mornings in Matthew, by Tammy Fleming.

Passport to the Land of Enough—Revised Edition, by Joel Nagel.

Prophets I—The Voices of Yahweh, by G. Steve Kinnard.

Prophets II—The Prophets of the Assyrian Period, by G. Steve Kinnard.

Prophets III—The Prophets of the Babylonian and Persion Periods, by G. Steve Kinnard.

Return to Sender—When There's Nowhere Left to Go but Home, by Guy Hammond.

Romans—The Heart Set Free, by Gordon Ferguson.

Revelation Revealed—Keys to Unlocking the Mysteries of Revelation, by Gordon Ferguson.

Spiritual Leadership for Women, Jeanie Shaw, Editor.

The Call of the Wise—An Introduction and Index of Proverbs, by G. Steve Kinnard.

The Cross of the Savior—From the Perspective of Jesus..., by Mark Templer.

The Final Act—A Biblical Look at End-Time Prophecy, by G. Steve Kinnard.

The Gospel of Matthew—The Crowning of the King, by G. Steve Kinnard.

The Letters of James, Peter, John, Jude—Life to the Full, by Douglas Jacoby.

The Lion Has Roared—An Exposition of Amos, by Douglas Jacoby.

The Seven People Who Help You to Heaven, by Sam Laing.

The Spirit—Presense & Power, Sense & Nonsense, by Douglas Jacoby.

Thrive—Using Psalms to Help You Flourish, by Douglas Jacoby.

What Happens After We Die? by Douglas Jacoby.

World Changers—The History of the Church in the Book of Acts, by Gordon Ferguson.

Marriage and Family

A Lifetime of Love—Building and Growing Your Marriage, by Al and Gloria Baird

Building Emotional Intimacy in Your Marriage, by Jeff and Florence Schachinger.

Hot and Holy—God's Plan for Exciting Sexual Intimacy in Marriage, by Sam Laing.

Faith and Finances, by Patrick Blair.

Friends & Lovers—Marriage as God Designed It, by Sam and Geri Laing.

Mighty Man of God—A Return to the Glory of Manhood, by Sam Laing.

Pure the Journey—A Radical Journey to a Pure Heart, by David and Robin Weidner.

Raising Awesome Kids—Being the Most Important Influence..., by Sam/Geri Laing.

Principle-Centered Parenting, by Douglas and Vicki Jacoby.

The Essential 8 Principles of a Growing Christian Marriage, by Sam and Geri Laing.

The Essential 8 Principles of a Strong Family, by Sam and Geri Laing.

Warrior—A Call to Every Man Everywhere, by Sam Laing.

For additional books go to
www.ipibooks.com

www.ingramcontent.com/pod-product-compliance
Lightning Source LLC
Chambersburg PA
CBHW021645120626
46545CB00002B/719